Encounters With Christ

Mark E. Moore

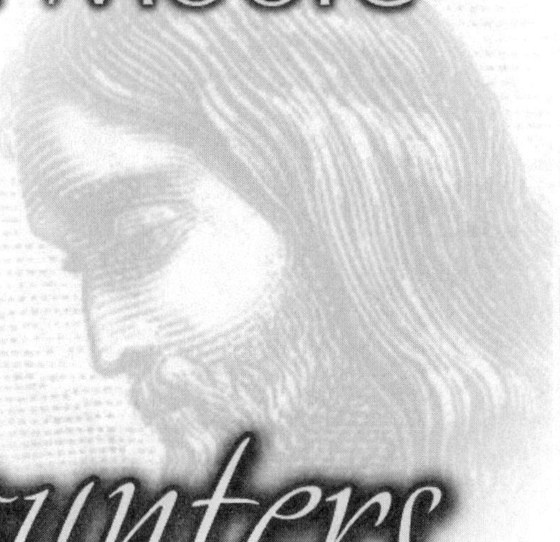

Encounters With Christ

A Call To Commitment

COLLEGE PRESS
PUBLISHING COMPANY
JOPLIN, MISSOURI

2nd Printing 2004
College Press Publishing Company
On the web at www.collegepress.com
Toll-free order line 1-800-289-3300

Printed and Bound in the
United States of America

Cover Design by Mark A. Cole

Library of Congress Cataloging-in-Publication Data

Moore, Mark E. (Mark Edward), 1963-
Encounters with Christ: a call to commitment/Mark E. Moore.
p. cm.
Includes bibliographical references.
ISBN 0-89900-874-7 (pbk.)
1. Jesus Christ—Biography—Public life—Meditations. I. Title
BT340.M66 2001
232.9'5—dc21

2001028655

To Josh and Megan

More than all my studies you two
have taught me about faith in Jesus.
Indeed, "The kingdom of heaven
belongs to such as these."

Table of Contents

Introduction

This is a book about Jesus. More specifically it introduces every person he encountered. There are sinners and apostles, enemies, and outcasts. Some come with a question, others with an accusation. Many are embraced, others rebuffed. Each shows, in his or her own way, how they met Jesus and the result of their encounter. Caution: As each vignette unfolds, you might find yourself somewhere in the scene, perhaps at Jesus' feet, or perhaps even up in his face. Among these many stories you may well find your own.

In essence, this book is a guide to help you navigate through your own encounter with Christ. He bids you come, with empty hands and broken hearts . . . come. Don't worry about your past, or your future. Once you accept the invitation, these all belong to him. All you have time to worry about now is believing. This will demand all of your energy, it will cost all of your earthly resources, it will consume your every waking moment. You see, Jesus doesn't merely want to be an addendum to a reasonably well-lived life. He demands to be Lord. He doesn't invite us to a church but to a pilgrimage. He beckons you to be his servant, student, friend, and bride. What's to be gained? Just a pearl — a treasure, forgiveness, a temple, a Lord, a husband, a country, Sabbath — Jesus himself, Jesus alone.

Throughout the book you will be directed to resources for further reading. Those which indicate they are available in electronic form from College Press are short outlines and studies that may be purchased to supplement this book.

Note: The chart on the following page categorizes these 83 encounters with Jesus by the nature of the person Jesus met (friends, seekers, opponents, outcasts or the infirm), as well as by the nature of the encounter. That is, what did Jesus teach through this meeting (faith, reversal in the kingdom, compassion, or Jesus' identity)? This chart functions as a guide to the book as well as an overview of Jesus' priorities for your own life.

Encounters with Christ

		Faith			Reversal				Compassion	Jesus' Identity	
		Trust	Money	Following	Kingdom	Outcasts	Sabbath/ Rituals	Cross first/last	How	Who	Power
Friends	The Baptist				22					2,22	
	Apostles/ disciples	33,80,81	50	10,30,46,49,72, 74,82,83	38,64	15		35,60,69,70	56	4,34,36,71,80,81	25,29,56
Seekers	Crowds			30						63,78	28
	Individuals	8	59	59	6						
Enemies	Family	40			24					1,5	
	Nazareth					9				9	
	Pharisees/ Sadducees	33		39	16		16,18,19,31,51	54,66	47,58	41,43,45,52,53, 65,75,76	73
	Herod									53,77	
	Satan									3	
Outcasts	Women (Noble)		67	48			51	68	21	79	27
	Women (Sinful)	23,32							42	7	
	Sinners					55,62					
	Gentiles	20,32									
Sick	Demoniac	37									11,26
	Sick	14,44,61					17,19,51		13,57	14,17	12

Encounters with Christ

The Early Years and Jesus' First Ministry

1 What Does God Look Like Going through Puberty? 1

{Luke 2:46-49; § 18-19}*

After three days they found him in the temple courts, sitting among the teachers, listening to them and asking them questions. Everyone who heard him was amazed at his understanding and his answers. When his parents saw him, they were astonished. His mother said to him, "Son, why have you treated us like this? Your father and I have been anxiously searching for you." "Why were you searching for me?" he asked. "Didn't you know I had to be in my Father's house?"

The question is not so much, "Does Jesus look like God?" but "Does God look like Jesus?" Yahweh came in the flesh to reveal himself for who he really was. So what does that look like? Answer: Jesus. God looks like Jesus when he raises the dead, walks on water, preaches, cries, and challenges the religious leaders. Here's the real shock: God even looks like Jesus as a 12-year-old boy.

This story is broader than the Bible. That is to say, describing a hero's childhood was a common literary device in Greek biographical writing. However, Greek writers didn't tell everything about the boy. They were not particularly interested in his hobbies or playground pals. Rather, they concentrated on some event early in puberty. This is an important time in the boy's life as he transitions into manhood. Now, the question the Greeks asked of the text was, "Did the boy exhibit in puberty the kind of character he would develop in manhood?" Again, these stories are not told merely for historical interest. They wanted to know if the boy prefigured the man.

In Jesus' case, the question is even more interesting, "Did the boy-God look like the God-man?" With that in mind, we come back to the text. Jesus enters the temple for the very first time. (Until now he had been too young). He is obviously enamored with what he saw. You would be too if you strolled through Herod's temple. Josephus describes it as lavishly ornate, covered with gold, and streaming with people. The biblical text of Leviticus came alive in these sacred

---

*The number following the symbol (§) indicates the section number of this incident in my two-volume *Chronological Life of Christ*. This will allow the reader to reference each section for further study.

precincts — blood flowed and smoke rose. Young Jesus now sees what before he had only read about and smelled from the outside. He must have been keenly interested in the Passover lambs. It was almost as if he could feel their suffering.

Jesus is so enthralled with it all that he fails to notice his parents' departure. They left when the feast was officially over; Jesus hangs around for the day of teaching that followed. Mary and Joseph don't notice his absence until the caravan beds down for the night. Since women and men traveled separately this is not such a shock. Jesus was at that transitional age when he might be found with the women or with the men. When he is found with neither, they bolt back to Jerusalem. Mary's heart is racing faster than her feet.

On the third day Jesus is found. He is sitting with the prominent teachers, asking and answering questions. This was the normal posture for a rabbinic student. The Doctors were amazed at this prodigy, and probably more so when they met his peasant parents. He had no pedigree that would predict this kind of genius. The problem was, they had yet to meet Jesus' real father.

Mary, like any other mother, explodes with frustrated relief. "Son, why have you treated us like this? Your father and I have been frantically searching for you!" Jesus' answer is classic. Remember, these are the first recorded words of Jesus and they answer this question: "Does the boy-God look like the God-man?" He says, "Why were you searching for me? Didn't you know it was necessary for me to be *amidst that which belongs to my Father*?" This is a difficult phrase to pin down with precision. It could mean, "In the temple." It could mean, "about my Father's business." Whatever else it might mean, certainly it means, "Like Father like Son." God looks like Jesus, even in puberty. He is his Father's child. This story must preface all other encounters with Christ. To meet Jesus is to touch the very face of God.

Further Reading: Philippians 2:1-11.

Ponderable Questions: In what ways did Jesus look like God at age twelve? How would these characteristics develop in his manhood? How could you develop those same characteristics in your own life? What do you think "my Father's business" meant to Jesus?

Considerations for Prayer: Sing "Make Me Like You, Lord." Pray through your itinerary, asking God to infuse his priorities into yours.

Was Jesus Baptized for the Remission of Sins?

{Matthew 3:13-17; § 24}

Then Jesus came from Galilee to the Jordan to be baptized by John. But John tried to deter him, saying, "I need to be baptized by you, and do you come to me?" Jesus replied, "Let it be so now; it is proper for us to do this to fulfill all righteousness." Then John consented. As soon as Jesus was baptized, he went up out of the water. At that moment heaven was opened, and he saw the Spirit of God descending like a dove and lighting on him. And a voice from heaven said, "This is my Son, whom I love; with him I am well pleased."

Jesus' baptism is big. Obviously, when the sky is torn open, it's a significant day. More than that, the Holy Spirit showed up in the form of a dove lighting on Jesus. Even the Father got into the act by booming from heaven, "This is my Son, whom I love . . ." We have, in one compressed moment, the movement of the entire Trinity. That's huge!

It was indeed big, but precisely what happened when Jesus was baptized? Some have suggested that he *became* the Son of God in that instance. Nonsense! He was as much God at his birth as he was at his baptism. Nevertheless, it does point out the fact that *something* significant happened. Was it that Jesus received the Holy Spirit? Was it here that his ministry began? Or is there something bigger than both of these?

This was the baptism of John. Like Christian baptism, it was for "repentance for the forgiveness of sins" (Mark 1:4; Acts 2:38). Jesus, like thousands of others, came to receive this initiatory rite. Everyone else who came was immersed for their sins. They were accepting his message of the incoming kingdom by repenting. When Jesus came, it must have looked like he was doing the very same thing. Perhaps that's why John objected, "I should be baptized by *you*, not you by me!" Obviously Jesus was not accepting the message of the soon-coming kingdom. He was its king, announcing its presence. Furthermore, Jesus had no personal sins from which to repent. So something *is* different in his immersion from everyone else's.

Yet does this mean that Jesus was not baptized for the forgiveness of sins? This may sound ludicrous since Jesus had no personal sins to repent from. However, let's keep two things in mind. First, the Gospels tend to be written backwards. (Most biographies are.) That is, we already know how things wind up before we read chapter 1. Thus, these books are to be read with the end in mind. That is, every story should be seen in the shadow of the cross. Second, in Jewish culture and history, the leader of a nation or people frequently took responsibility for the actions of his/her citizens. Kings were responsible for citizens, fathers for children, and teachers for students. This is particularly true with repentance. Nehemiah repented for the sins of his people — sins that he, himself, did not commit. The same can be said for Ezra, Daniel, Isaiah, etc.

Thus Jesus' baptism could be understood by his countrymen as a corporate, rather than an individual, event. In other words, he was baptized for the sins of the nation. If this is so, then Jesus is making a bold assertion here. He claims to be the one true leader of Israel! No wonder God marked this coronation with a heavenly proclamation. Furthermore, Jesus' baptism now mirrors the cross, for in both, Jesus takes on the sins of the nation.

Yes, this is a huge event. Here Jesus begins his ministry and foreshadows the cross. Here he is empowered by the Holy Spirit. Here he is approved by God. And here he clarifies the course of his career. He will be the sin-bearer for his people. Like the Israelites of old, Jesus leads a new nation through the Jordan River into the promised land. He isn't merely a personal Lord, he is a national king. His baptism was his coronation; ours is our emigration. In Jesus' baptism God announced him as Son. In ours we are adopted into the family. In his, the Holy Spirit descended from above as a dove. In ours he stamps us internally as a fire branding our hearts with the ownership of Yahweh. In this act, Jesus prefigures our own pilgrimage.

Further Reading: Romans 6:4-7; "Baptism" — available in electronic form from College Press.

Ponderable Questions: What similar images run through Jesus' baptism, the cross, and our own baptism? In what ways did Jesus' baptism change the course of his ministry? How did your own baptism change the course of yours? How does this event announce the in-breaking of the kingdom?

Considerations for Prayer: Thank God for the atonement of Christ and how you were able to reenact Jesus' passion through your own immersion. Ask for wisdom to live up to your new identity.

Satan vs. Jesus

{Matthew 4:1-11; § 25}

Then Jesus was led by the Spirit into the desert to be tempted by the devil. After fasting forty days and forty nights, he was hungry. The tempter came to him and said, "If you are the Son of God, tell these stones to become bread." Jesus answered, "It is written: 'Man does not live on bread alone, but on every word that comes from the mouth of God.'" Then the devil took him to the holy city and had him stand on the highest point of the temple. "If you are the Son of God," he said, "throw yourself down. . . . Jesus answered him, "It is also written: 'Do not put the Lord your God to the test.'" Again, the devil took him to a very high mountain and showed him all the kingdoms of the world and their splendor. "All this I will give you," he said, "if you will bow down and worship me." Jesus said to him, "Away from me, Satan! For it is written: 'Worship the Lord your God, and serve him only.'" Then the devil left him, and angels came and attended him.

Some see this text as a mirror of the Christian experience. Leaning on Hebrews 4:15, they say, "Look how Jesus was tempted just like we are. He walked in our shoes. He feels our pain." This is not untrue. Here we find Jesus as earthly as he gets. He wrestles with the pangs of hunger as well as the schemes of the Devil. In this sense, Jesus understands our plight perfectly.

However, this text is deeper than our own experience. It plumbs depths where we do not belong. The nation of Israel was forged out of 40 years of wilderness wanderings. So too, Jesus' ministry is founded on forty days of fasting in the desert. His temptations here are not precisely like ours. For instance, consider turning rocks into bread. First of all, most of us probably don't wrestle with this particular temptation. Secondly, if someone did, in fact, turn stones into bread, we would wonder at the miracle, not cringe at the sin. How is it, then, that for Jesus this would have been a failure when for us it would be fantastic?

The answer is at the end of Jesus' ministry, not the beginning. Everything in the Gospels leads to Golgotha. If read in the shadow of the cross, these three temptations come into crystal clear focus. Satan is not tempting Jesus to lower himself by some moral degradation. He tempts Jesus to short-circuit the cross. For instance, Satan offers to give up the kingdoms of this world without a fight if Jesus will but bow. Again, if Jesus will dazzle the crowds with a divine display of power by jumping off the top of the temple, he can avoid the arduous task of slow self-disclosure. These are the shortcuts to the kingdom. The problem is obvious: Jesus could have the title of king without purity of purpose and perspective.

Even something as simple as turning stones to bread could subvert God's plan. Notice carefully Matthew's last sentence, "Angels came and attended him." This only happened one other time. It was not in a desert but a garden, yet there too he wrestled alone. Jesus will struggle with God's plan as he prays three times, "Let this cup pass from me." Had he waffled in the wilderness he would have crumbled in the garden. In both instances Jesus declined his divine prerogative so as to fully embrace the human predicament.

Jesus' encounter with the devil is telling. It provides us a model for our own spiritual warfare through the Word. Jesus didn't resist the devil with stellar self-control or clever argumentation. He relied on the power of God's word. We appreciate Jesus' showing us the way out of temptation. More important still, this text reminds us that the gravest danger is not moral failure. Jesus can deal with that. Our greatest danger is being derailed from the kingdom of the cross. When we pretend that there is an easier way, a way to avoid self-abnegation and suffering, we turn stones to bread. Even if it is adorned with success, any path that averts the cross is ultimately perilous.

Further Reading: Hebrews 4:14-16; 1 Corinthians 10:13.

Ponderable Questions: What could/would have happened if Jesus submitted to the Devil's offer in the wilderness? Was that a real possibility? Jesus resisted temptation by quoting Scripture as well as by a single-minded focus on God's will. How would these help you in your present temptations?

Considerations for Prayer: Pray through the Lord's Prayer, particularly asking God not to abandon you in evil. Ask the Holy Spirit to convict you of sin in your life and show you the way out.

What Can You Find under a Fig Tree?

{John 1:35-41,45-51; § 28}

Andrew, Simon Peter's brother, was one of the two who heard what John had said and who had followed Jesus. The first thing Andrew did was to find his brother Simon and tell him, "We have found the Messiah" (that is, the Christ). . . . Philip found Nathanael and told him, "We have found the one Moses wrote about in the Law, and about whom the prophets also wrote—Jesus of Nazareth, the son of Joseph." "Nazareth! Can anything good come from there?" Nathanael asked. "Come and see," said Philip. When Jesus saw Nathanael approaching, he said of him, "Here is a true Israelite, in whom there is nothing false." "How do you know me?" Nathanael asked. Jesus answered, "I saw you while you were still under the fig tree before Philip called you." Then Nathanael declared, "Rabbi, you are the Son of God; you are the King of Israel." Jesus said, ". . . I tell you the truth, you shall see heaven open, and the angels of God ascending and descending on the Son of Man."

The tumblers of the kingdom begin to fall into place. Jesus has been baptized by water in the Jordan and by fire in the desert. It is now time to gather a few followers. The first half-dozen are recruits from John's ministry. One of them is a man named Philip. His only real claim to fame is bringing people to Jesus (John 6:5-7; 12:20-22). He scampers off to tell his friend about this great discovery. "We have found the Messiah," he cries, "the one Moses and the prophets wrote about." Nathanael, with cavalier nonchalance replies, "Nazareth! Can anything good come from there?!" You can't really argue with illogical prejudice, so Philip simply invites him to "come and see."

Before they get close to him, Jesus calls out to Nathanael, "Here is a true Israelite, in whom there is nothing false." (This is, of course, something of a paradox since the progenitor of the Israelites was a deceiver in name and character.) On the surface it looks like a nice compliment. But Nathanael receives it as much more. He is amazed that Jesus already knows him. "Oh, that's nothing," Jesus replies, "I saw you while you were still under the fig tree before Philip called you." Again, this appears to be a rather unimpressive identification. There were fig trees all over Palestine and they were favorite places to rest from the blistering sun. Yet Nathanael reacts as if he has just had an epiphany, "Rabbi, you are the Son of God; you are the king of Israel!"

Nathanael's reaction is, frankly, perplexing. This is the greatest declaration of Jesus' identity to date. It comes before his first miracle in Cana, before the cleansing of the temple in Jerusalem, before any great sermon, before the plethora of miraculous healings. This confession is based on a seemingly simple identification of Nathanael. There must be a deeper current running through the text. While we may not be able to understand everything going on here, there are a few clear streams. (1) Nathanael is an honest man who, like most of us, stands in a dishonest generation as well as a deceitful genealogy. (2) He was sitting under a fig tree, which figuratively represented Israel's Messianic hopes (cf. Micah 4:4; Luke 13:6-9). (3) Jesus knew who he was, including his aspirations and motives, before ever meeting him. These three streams converge and culminate in a confession of Christ. When Jesus exposed Nathanael's heart, he also loosed his lips to sing the praises of this Galilean. There was something about Jesus' knowing Nathanael that revealed himself as Messiah. At once his dreams materialized into the vision of this man who stood before him. Nathanael's eyes opened wide. Jesus promised he would see much more. Like Jacob long ago, Nathanael's vision of Jesus would stretch to heaven, lined with angels. This was only the beginning of what Nathanael would see in Jesus.

So what is the conclusion? For many, Nathanael is autobiographical. Reading his story is like looking in a mirror. Perhaps he is you. Perhaps you have honestly searched for God and, upon encountering Christ, you suddenly, intuitively knew that he's the one you've been looking for all your life! How did you know? It didn't take a miracle or a prophecy. It didn't require a sermon or some supernatural vision. When we encounter Christ, *because* he knows us for who we really are, we recognize him for who he truly is. Only the Son of God can see the longings hidden deep in our hearts. One who knows us so well is one we simply must follow.

Further Reading: John 1:35-51; Psalm 139.

Ponderable Questions: Describe how you first came to know Jesus. Was your first encounter similar to Nathanael's? How do you feel about the fact that Jesus knows you as well as he does? How does (or should), his intimate knowledge of us shape our relationship with him?

Considerations for Prayer: Sing "Jesus, Jesus, Jesus." Ask Jesus to make you as free from "guile" as Nathanael. Confess to him your deepest longings and ask him to satisfy them with himself.

It's Party Time!

{John 2:3-8; § 29}

When the wine was gone, Jesus' mother said to him, "They have no more wine." "Dear woman, why do you involve me?" Jesus replied. "My time has not yet come." His mother said to the servants, "Do whatever he tells you." Nearby stood six stone water jars, the kind used by the Jews for ceremonial washing, each holding from twenty to thirty gallons. Jesus said to the servants, "Fill the jars with water"; so they filled them to the brim. Then he told them, "Now draw some out and take it to the master of the banquet."

We're not merely talking about a couple of cakes and a few bowls of mints. Jewish weddings typically lasted for a full week. They were filled with banquets, dancing, laughter, and song. Moreover, the celebration was not simply over a cute young couple who had fallen in love. Rather, Middle Eastern weddings were an alliance between two families through a marriage contract. These social/political unions were critically important.

Jesus, who has been gone for the better part of a year, steps back into the scene of his biological family and soon finds himself embroiled in hometown politics. The groom's family miscalculated the amount of wine needed for the celebration. This is more than an embarrassing faux pas. Such neglect could cause serious offense to the bride's family, resulting in significant ramifications.

Mary is asked to help. Apparently someone thought she had access to some resources that could provide more wine. She, of course, goes straight to her oldest son, the leader of their clan. When she informs Jesus of the predicament, she doesn't actually ask for him to help, but the implication is clear. She is requesting Jesus to intervene on behalf of the groom's family. Here we need to observe two things. First, Mary is not necessarily asking Jesus to perform a miracle. He could probably provide sufficient wine from the resources in the apostolic purse. Furthermore, since this is the first miracle recorded in John's Gospel, you wouldn't expect Mary to anticipate such divine intervention in a mundane affair. Second, if he does help, that would greatly increase the clout of Jesus' family. In social science terms, Mary's family would become patrons and this wedding party their clients. This would no doubt delight Mary.

It is time for Jesus to get on with his ministry. He has a new family now, and to become the patron of the wedding would be a step backward, not forward, in his Messianic career. At the same time he does need to honor his mother. His dilemma is more serious than it appears on the surface. The Scriptures compel him to honor his earthly mother. His calling compels him to honor his heavenly Father. Solution: turn water to wine. In one fell swoop Jesus honors his mother *and* opens a new chapter in his Messianic career.

Here is where it gets good. The servants fill six water jars to the brim. Before they can say "Mogen David," they have upwards of 180 gallons of wine. No wonder they called Jesus a "wine-bibber"! In anyone's book this is a bit excessive. Why so much wine? Well, as Jesus' mother fades from the scene, the kingdom comes clearly into view. Let's back up for a bird's-eye view of the whole scene.

We must remember that John records a mere seven miracles. In other words, he is not trying to overwhelm his readers with the bulk of Jesus' wondrous deeds. He selects them carefully and describes them specifically so that they preach about the kingdom of God. They are, so to speak, enacted parables. Every one of them carries an important lesson about the nature of the kingdom. This first one introduces John's audience to a core concept of the kingdom: It is a party of excessive proportions. Wine and weddings represent joyful celebration. The point of the story is anchored in one hundred and eighty gallons — that's enough blessing to bathe in! Our initial encounter with Jesus is an invitation to a wedding where the wine flows freely. He wants to transform your life into an extraordinary event filled with joy, wine, love, and dance. Even though your stock has run dry, Jesus invites you to a glut of celebration. In Christ there is no such thing as a shower of blessing. It is a deluge! ***Le Chaim!***

Further Reading: Revelation 19:6-9; "Mary" — available in electronic form from College Press.

Ponderable Questions: In what ways were you taught that being a Christian was something other than a life of joy? Do you still subconsciously believe or act like the kingdom is less than unmitigated celebration? List the things our Lord lavishes on us that are worth jubilation.

Considerations for Prayer: Celebrate!

Nicodemus and New Birth

{John 3:1-6; § 32}

Now there was a man of the Pharisees named Nicodemus, a member of the Jewish ruling council. He came to Jesus at night and said, "Rabbi, we know you are a teacher who has come from God. For no one could perform the miraculous signs you are doing if God were not with him." In reply Jesus declared, "I tell you the truth, no one can see the kingdom of God unless he is born again." "How can a man be born when he is old?" Nicodemus asked. "Surely he cannot enter a second time into his mother's womb to be born!" Jesus answered, "I tell you the truth, no one can enter the kingdom of God unless he is born of water and the Spirit. Flesh gives birth to flesh, but the Spirit gives birth to spirit."

He is sharply dressed, highly cultured and well educated. After all, he is a member of the ruling council, a Pharisee among Pharisees. He loves God and apparently takes a liking to Jesus (cf. John 7:50-52; 19:38-39). He could spend his time with any of the elite. But on this evening, he weaves his way through the streets of Jerusalem to locate this peasant from Galilee. Jesus had attracted a fair bit of attention with his display in the temple and his healings on the side. John 2:23-24 says, "Many people saw the miraculous signs he was doing and believed in his name. But Jesus would not entrust himself to them, for he knew all men." Nicodemus falls into this lot.

He comes with a confession. It's a good one too: "Jesus, we know you are from God . . . ." Now that's a very nice thing to say. So why does Jesus' response seem out of sorts? "No one can see the kingdom of God unless he is born again." Jesus insults this dignified leader who comes to him with a compliment. Moreover, Nicodemus has said nothing about the kingdom. Conclusion: Jesus is not responding to Nicodemus' words but to his heart. His abrupt, and perhaps discourteous, response arises out of passion, not contempt.

If Jesus does "come from God" as Nicodemus suggests, the logical conclusion is that he is the Messiah, ushering in the kingdom. As a ruler of Israel, Nicodemus would expect to be central to this divine enterprise. It is almost as if Nicodemus is saying, "Jesus, I know who you are and what you're up to. Now, when do we get started?"

Nicodemus's heart is right. It's his perception of the kingdom that needs work. He was surely convinced that all his service to God, his education, experience, clout, and prestige, would be a great asset to Jesus' program. Surprise! Not only does Jesus not need our fine resume, if we are to enter the kingdom, we need to scrap it! We start fresh when we enter the kingdom. With nothing in our hands, no medals on our chest, no billfolds, credentials, kudos, or degrees. How, then, does one enter the kingdom? We must be born again, literally born "from above." This is a work of God, not of man. Watch.

Being born again is a mysterious transformation of the *Spirit* (vv. 5-8), when one looks upon *Jesus* lifted up on the cross (vv. 14-15). All this is from *God* who "loved the world" with reckless abandon (v. 16). What a wonderful Trinitarian text! New birth in the kingdom comes from the fullness of God. It is larger than life. Even one as impressive as Nicodemus had nothing to add, nothing to offer. Indeed, "we are saved by grace through faith and that not of ourselves lest anyone should boast" (Eph. 2:8-9, paraphrase). The reason we enter as newborns is because nothing of our old life is relevant to the new. That which earned us honor before is now merely a distraction. Our religious pedigrees allow us to pretend that we come to God with something to offer. The truth is, unless we come humbled and barren, with empty hands and open hearts, then access to the kingdom is denied. There are no shortcuts, no alternate routes. All must pass the way of the cross.

Further Reading: John 1:1-21; Philippians 3:7-11, "John 3:5" — available in electronic form from College Press.

Ponderable Questions: What kinds of things do people tend to trust in to gain approval from God? How do you see yourself, or the church in general, wrestling with this idea of righteousness by pedigree? Why is our own goodness so worthless for impressing God?

Considerations for Prayer: Offer up to God your own good works, not as a gift to be cherished but as a distraction to be abandoned. Express to Christ your utter faith in him alone.

What Would You Do for Living Water?

{John 4:10-14,39-42; § 35}

Jesus answered her, "If you knew the gift of God and who it is that asks you for a drink, you would have asked him and he would have given you living water." "Sir," the woman said, "you have nothing to draw with and the well is deep. Where can you get this living water? Are you greater than our father Jacob, who gave us the well and drank from it himself, as did also his sons and his flocks and herds?" Jesus answered, "Everyone who drinks this water will be thirsty again, but whoever drinks the water I give him will never thirst. Indeed, the water I give him will become in him a spring of water welling up to eternal life." . . . Many of the Samaritans from that town believed in him because of the woman's testimony, "He told me everything I ever did." So when the Samaritans came to him, they urged him to stay with them, and he stayed two days. And because of his words many more became believers. They said to the woman, "We no longer believe just because of what you said; now we have heard for ourselves, and we know that this man really is the Savior of the world."

She was a mess! The kind of woman that gets gossiped about. It's no surprise that at high noon she finds herself walking to the well alone. The Bible does not say she is friendless, although that's not too great a stretch. A woman with a live-in lover and five previous husbands doesn't tend to endear herself to the quilting club.

As she approaches Jacob's well, she sees a Galilean Jew sitting on the edge. His presence, no doubt, reminds her that she is precariously alone. She is a bit more than slightly uncomfortable. The well isn't that big. He will be hard to ignore — *especially* when he asks her for a drink! After she picked her jaw up off the ground, she asked, "Why are you even talking to me, a woman and a Samaritan?" Why indeed?! Precisely because she is a person worth saving in spite of her history.

Her question opens the floodgate. Out pours a discussion on living water. Oh what she would do for living water! In Palestine this is more than a religious symbol. Living water — an active stream or spring — was the source of life for agrarian peasants. Living water would mean clean drinking water and fertile gardens. It would reduce her labor and increase her net worth. It would provide refreshment, rest, pleasure, and power. To be sure, she understands what living water means. She just doesn't believe Jesus can provide it.

She is a clever gal. She takes Jesus to task and soon finds that his prophetic knowledge is deeper than she thought. So is his offer of living water. He is not just offering a temporary fix to an arduous existence. He is offering forgiveness of sins and spiritual refreshment. Now that's worth shoutin' about! She scampers off to town and attracts a crowd with this simple statement: "Come, see a man who told me everything I ever did." With her past you might expect this to engender a good bit of interest. By the time the townsfolk walk to the well, Jesus' own disciples have returned to him with lunch. When he sees the crowd marching across the fields of grain, he says to his disciples, "Do you not say, 'Four months more and then the harvest'? I tell you, open your eyes and look at the fields! They are ripe for harvest. Even now the reaper draws his wages, even now he harvests the crop for eternal life, so that the sower and reaper may be glad together." A great harvest it was. By the end of the day, these Samaritans confessed of Jesus, "This man really is the Savior of the World."

This story, as it stands, is fantastic. Yet read alongside chapter three it is grander still. Who could miss the connection between the Samaritan woman and Nicodemus? He, a man from the upper echelons of Jewish society. She, a Samaritan woman of ill repute. He was prized and praised. She was pawned and scandalized. He had clout; she had scars. **YET**, Nicodemus came at night and was told to be reborn in water; Jesus met her at midday and offered her a drink. She became an instant success as an evangelist; Nicodemus ever remains on the sidelines of Jesus' movement. His associates wind up crucifying Jesus; hers hail him as Savior of the world (John 4:42). Truly the wise of this world are foolish to God, but God takes the foolish things and exalts them. Please don't pity the woman at the well, for she is beloved by Jesus. Nor should you pity yourself. Unless, of course you sit on the Sanhedrin.

Can lowly people come to Jesus? No. They don't have to. He has already come to them.

Further Reading: John 4:1-42; Acts 8:4-8; Isaiah 55:1-2; "Samaritans" — available in electronic form from College Press.

Ponderable Questions: Are you more like Nicodemus or the woman at the well? Recount a time when you felt unworthy to come to Jesus but he received you anyway. What people around you feel rejected by Christians whom Jesus could embrace through you?

Considerations for Prayer: Ask Jesus to quench your thirst. Ask him to open your eyes to the Samaritan women all around you and to the fields that are white unto harvest.

Encounters with Christ

The Galilean Ministry

8 Rich Guys Don't Always Get What They Want 

{John 4:46b-52; § 38}

There was a certain royal official whose son lay sick at Capernaum. When this man heard that Jesus had arrived in Galilee from Judea, he went to him and begged him to come and heal his son, who was close to death. "Unless you people see miraculous signs and wonders," Jesus told him, "you will never believe." The royal official said, "Sir, come down before my child dies." Jesus replied, "You may go. Your son will live." The man took Jesus at his word and departed. While he was still on the way, his servants met him with the news that his boy was living. When he inquired as to the time when his son got better, they said to him, "The fever left him yesterday at the seventh hour."

He came twenty miles to find this faith healer. Undoubtedly a man of his stature did not travel alone. His entourage encounters Christ with a question: "Will you please come to Capernaum to heal my son?" Such a request of an itinerant peasant preacher is quite a compliment coming from this nobleman. Yet rather than jumping at the opportunity, Jesus rebukes this sign-seeking crowd: "Unless you people see miraculous signs and wonders you will never believe!"

Pardon me for saying so, but this seems a bit harsh. Here this guy's kid is laying on his deathbed and Jesus goes off on him. What did he do that was so bad? Sure the nobleman asks Jesus to travel 20 miles to help his son. What father wouldn't? Perhaps he appears a bit selfish seeing as how hundreds in Cana needed Jesus just as badly. But you can't blame the guy for making the request. He was, after all, going out on a limb for a good cause.

Furthermore, is the crowd's curiosity such a terrible thing? Who wouldn't want to see a miracle? What horde of humanity is less curious? Oh sure, there are more spiritual things to seek than signs. But really, are we so different? Perhaps that's precisely the point. We find ourselves peculiarly present in the pages of this text. We seek Jesus all right — often for these same wrong reasons. We come for what we can get out of him, not because we are drawn to his person. It is not that he is unwilling to heal us, unwilling to lavish his power on our sick children. On the contrary, he has proven time and again just how gracious he is. What he finds offensive, however, is when we come to receive instead of coming to believe. It is somewhat like a bride who gladly gives herself to her husband but would be scandalized if propositioned in her wedding dress by a stranger. How we approach another may well determine the response we receive. The nobleman believes Jesus can help him and comes with a request. What he lacks is real faith — a faith to follow Jesus, to submit his life to his Lordship. It is one thing to need Jesus; it is quite another to receive him.

Verse 54 says, "This was the second miraculous sign that Jesus performed." Since John only records seven of these signs, each one is theologically loaded. We're not just reading a quaint tale of Jesus' power. No, this is an enacted parable that screams about the kingdom of God. This paradigmatic episode instructs believers how to live in the kingdom. Not surprisingly the focus of the story is faith. It is found at its pinnacle (v. 48) and its conclusion (vv. 53-54). The point is this: when we come to Jesus, he expects us to come with faith. There must be more than mere "belief" in his power. It has to do with the depth of our relationship with him. He is an extraordinary healer and a powerful Lord. This is to our advantage, for sure. However, he is not some "sugar daddy" that doles out miracles every time we find ourselves in trouble. Jesus was not impressed by the nobleman's pedigree, nor is he impressed by ours. Without faith it is impossible to please God. Without faith we dare not approach Jesus. He demands allegiance to his person, not merely acceptance of his power.

Further Reading: Hebrews 11:1-38.

Ponderable Questions: What have you done lately that would impress Jesus with faith? Does your prayer life reflect this man's request without real relationship? Of all the people you know personally, who has the deepest, most active faith? Is there some step of faith that Jesus has been urging you to take that you have been procrastinating about?

Considerations for Prayer: "Lord I believe. . . . Help me in my unbelief."

Hometown Boy Thinks He's a Prophet

{Luke 4:16-19,21,24,28-30; § 39}

He went to Nazareth, where he had been brought up, and on the Sabbath day he went into the synagogue, as was his custom. And he stood up to read. The scroll of the prophet Isaiah was handed to him. Unrolling it, he found the place where it is written: "The Spirit of the Lord is on me, / because he has anointed me / to preach good news to the poor. / He has sent me to proclaim freedom for the prisoners / and recovery of sight for the blind, / to release the oppressed, / to proclaim the year of the Lord's favor." . . . He began by saying to them, "Today this scripture is fulfilled in your hearing." . . . "I tell you the truth," he continued, "no prophet is accepted in his hometown. . . . All the people in the synagogue were furious when they heard this. They got up, drove him out of the town, and took him to the brow of the hill on which the town was built, in order to throw him down the cliff. But he walked right through the crowd and went on his way.

"A prophet has no honor in his own home town." This proverb may not be true in every case, but it sure was true with Jesus. He arrives in Nazareth somewhat of a local hero. He's been away for the better part of a year. During that time he has cleaned out the temple in Jerusalem and healed the masses in Judea. He has gathered a small band of disciples and huge crowds travel long distances to hear him preach. As you can imagine, his homecoming was quite the event. Old friends were united, Sabbath School teachers were delighted to see the fame of their own native son. Of course, he was asked to preach that Sabbath in the synagogue. That's when the trouble began.

As his text he chose a passage from Isaiah 61:1-2. It comes as no surprise that his passage has strong Messianic overtones. This Galilean contingent would have liked that. So far so good. Things went south in a hurry, however, when he claimed the text was talking about *him*! They were scandalized when Jesus said, "Today this scripture is fulfilled in your hearing." The blatant audacity! To claim that a particular Bible verse was written about you! You can almost still hear the murmuring that swept through the congregation. The rumble wafted over the front pew and broke out onto the platform in open aggression. Jesus meets their challenge head on. First he puts them in their place with this proverb about a physician healing himself. Then he scandalized them by applying the Elijah and Elisha accounts to their own place and time. Essentially Jesus is saying, "Just as God abandoned Israel for foreigners in Elijah and Elisha's day, so he will do it again through me!"

This talk about Gentiles being blessed instead of the Jews was not so well received. To suggest that he was the Messiah was bad enough. But to insinuate that God's people would miss him while the pagans would accept him was entirely uncalled for! Infuriated, they tried to do him in right then and there. Unwittingly, they fulfilled the very prediction that so angered them.

This message of Gentile inclusion wasn't popular. But Jesus wasn't the only one to preach it. Matthew says basically the same thing when he applies Isaiah 9:1-2 to Jesus (cf. Matt. 4:15-16). Luke, who records this story, heard Paul say to his Jewish audience on more than one occasion, "I'm leaving you now and preaching to the Gentiles." With a clap of his sandals and a small cloud of dust he was off.

How ironic it is that in his home congregation Jesus predicted his ministry to the world. How ironic it is that the very people who had "first dibs" on Jesus tried to do away with him. This irony is echoed in John 1:11, "He came to that which was his own, but his own did not receive him." What a terribly sad verse for these insiders. Yet what good news for the Gentiles and beggars, the outcasts and disenfranchised. Jesus breaks every social, economic, and ethnic boundary as he reaches out to hurting people. If we do any less, can we claim to be his followers? In your mind's eye, sit yourself down in the pew at your church. Look around. Do you see the "hometown folks"? Or do you see the widow of Zarephath and Naaman? Now before you excoriate your leaders or preachers, please remember that you alone are responsible for who sits next to you in church. You are the one responsible for the foreigners. They are not nearly as distant as they used to be. If you want Jesus on your right, you may want to have a leper on your left.

Further Reading: Acts 10-11; "Cornelius," and "Synagogue" — available in electronic form from College Press.

Ponderable Questions: Why did Jesus' synagogue get so upset with him? What kinds of people would traditionally not be welcomed in church? Are they welcomed in yours? What are you actively doing to see that they are? Why is it important that we pursue ministry to the "outcasts"?

Considerations for Prayer: "Lord give us eyes to see people as you do, hearts (and perhaps fists) that pound for their inclusion, and wisdom not to be hurtful in the process."

What a Catch!

{Luke 5:4-10; § 41}

> When he had finished speaking, he said to Simon, "Put out into deep water, and let down the nets for a catch." Simon answered, "Master, we've worked hard all night and haven't caught anything. But because you say so, I will let down the nets." When they had done so, they caught such a large number of fish that their nets began to break. So they signaled their partners in the other boat to come and help them, and they came and filled both boats so full that they began to sink. When Simon Peter saw this, he fell at Jesus' knees and said, "Go away from me, Lord; I am a sinful man!" For he and all his companions were astonished at the catch of fish they had taken, and so were James and John, the sons of Zebedee, Simon's partners. Then Jesus said to Simon, "Don't be afraid; from now on you will catch men."

They had already followed Jesus for the better part of a year. In all likelihood, these fishermen had been disciples of John the Baptist before that. They were familiar with radical preaching, large crowds, and miraculous signs. But nothing in their résumé prepared them for this. If you asked them, "Have you sacrificially followed Jesus?" they likely would be insulted that you even asked the question!

You know the story. Jesus turns Peter's boat into a pulpit. Peter is still sulking after a bad night of fishing. They caught absolutely nothing! What's worse, these guys are not tinkering with a hobby, they are trying to make a living. After following Jesus for ten months, there were surely bills to pay.

Jesus tells Peter to throw the nets overboard for one last attempt. What a stupid suggestion! They were in the wrong part of the lake, it was the wrong time of the day, and the nets had already been cleaned and repaired. This is a lot of work merely to humor the master. Nevertheless, when Jesus gave the command, Peter obeyed.

As he pulled up the net his muscles began to bulge . . . so did his eyes. He beckoned his partners who came to the rescue with a second boat. This was a catch of epic proportions! What a boon this was to Peter's business. You'd think Peter would be delighted . . . but he's not. He's on his knees, hip deep in squirming mackerel with this request: "Depart from me, Lord; I am a sinful man."

It was one thing for Jesus to turn water into wine. It was impressive when he gave sight to the blind. It was fascinating when he cast out demons. But this catch of fish was entirely different for Peter. Jesus was on Peter's turf. In Peter's own boat Jesus demonstrated that he was no mere magician, he was Lord of creation.

We tend to imagine that seeing Jesus would be a wonderful thing — terribly exhilarating! In the Scriptures, however, seeing Jesus for who he really is, is terribly terrifying! He is not tamed and will not be trifled with. He is neither safe nor predictable. What's worse, he won't leave you alone. Instead of granting Peter's request, he has his own certain demand: "Follow me, and I will make you a fisher of men." It wasn't enough that Peter had accompanied Jesus. Jesus demanded that he drop all his other allegiances, dreams, programs, and plans. Jesus has but one great grand gift to offer in its place: To take live captives from behind enemy lines. For a Christian, all else is avocation. Our singular, clear call, captured in this episode with Peter, is to seek and to save the lost.

Further Reading: Matthew 4:18-22; Revelation 1:12-18; "Apostles" — available in electronic form from College Press.

Ponderable Questions: Describe what you think it would really be like to see Jesus? How would you react? What are you presently doing to participate in "taking live captives"? Have you fully responded to Jesus' call to follow him? Has he called you vocationally?

Considerations for Prayer: Offer the Lord your net and boat. Listen carefully for further instructions.

A Funny Thing Happened in Church

{Mark 1:21-28; § 42}

They went to Capernaum, and when the Sabbath came, Jesus went into the synagogue and began to teach. The people were amazed at his teaching, because he taught them as one who had authority, not as the teachers of the law. Just then a man in their synagogue who was possessed by an evil spirit cried out, "What do you want with us, Jesus of Nazareth? Have you come to destroy us? I know who you are—the Holy One of God!" "Be quiet!" said Jesus sternly. "Come out of him!" The evil spirit shook the man violently and came out of him with a shriek. The people were all so amazed that they asked each other, "What is this? A new teaching—and with authority! He even gives orders to evil spirits and they obey him."

One fine Sabbath day Jesus was teaching in the synagogue of Capernaum. This metropolitan village had become his headquarters, so he was no stranger to the folks at church. Neither was the demoniac. He was boisterous, rude, and violent, all of which added to his reputation. When he came out of the shadows during the service, you could hear the collective gasp of the crowd roll across the room. Two heavyweights were about to collide. No doubt the air was thick with nervous energy. Suddenly this wild man exploded, "Ha! What do you want with us, Jesus of Nazareth? Have you come to destroy us? I know who you are — the Holy One of God!"

Under normal circumstances, with normal rabbis, there would be a flurry of exorcistic activity. There were always appropriate incantations and magical formulae used in an attempt to wrest a demon from its prey. Instead, Jesus simply turns to the demoniac and orders him to shut up and leave. BOOM! It was done. Just like that! There were no arguments or attacks. Granted, the demon shook him real hard as he slammed the door shut and shouted on his way out, but Dr. Luke notes that there were no serious injuries.

You can just imagine the shock of the crowd. In a day when exorcism involved complex rituals, Jesus' sole word of authority was staggering. It is really no great wonder his fame spread like shock waves across the hills and villas of Galilee. Furthermore, this was not the only incident when Jesus ordered demons around. In fact, Jesus' preaching, healing, and exorcisms form the tripod of his ministry.

What does all this mean? At the surface level it suggests that Jesus has spiritual power that the demons could identify but never compete with. It also means that his preaching was bolstered by exorcisms. After all, who wouldn't listen to the guy who just won the heavyweight bout? This is all good, but the purpose of this story runs deeper. When we read this portion of Jesus' biography chronologically, we line up several stories that must be seen together. As soon as Jesus declares the intent of his ministry (Luke 4:16-30) and chooses his first disciples (Mark 1:16-20), he has three significant encounters: The demoniac (Mark 1:21-28), sickness (Mark 1:29-34), and a leper (Mark 1:40-45). These three "categories" represent the major spiritual land mines of Jesus' day — demons, sickness, and uncleanness. In their eyes, each of these was caused by the devil's schemes, God's abandonment, or both. As a result, when Jesus faces off with the demon, he is making a full frontal assault on the works of the devil. The kingdom of God is here, and it has radical implications for the *modus operandi* of the devil. Obviously the kingdom is not fully manifested. However, it has a serious impact on the way life is lived in this satanically stained society. This little story is not a "way back then" kind of a tale. It belongs on the front page: Jesus has inaugurated the kingdom . . . serve notice to the forces of darkness. Through the power of Christ, we assault the work of the Evil One. No more does he have free rein; no more does he enjoy uncontested possession. Furthermore, Jesus' frontal assault is not through magic or superstitions. It is through the unmitigated raw power of his word alone. So then, when we preach the word of Christ, we stand where he stood on the front lines of spiritual mayhem, attacking the works of darkness. Where we stand with his word, we stand with his power extending a foray deep into enemy territory.

Further Reading: Luke 4:31b-37; Ephesians 6:10-18; "Demons" — available in electronic form from College Press.

Ponderable Questions: What do you know about spiritual warfare? How have you experienced it? What are our weapons? How is Satan attempting to destroy you? How does Jesus come to our rescue? What opportunities do you presently have to extend the rule of God into Satanic territory?

Considerations for Prayer: Pray for those you suspect are under spiritual attack. Ask Jesus to help you strap on your armor.

No Mother-in-Law Jokes, Please

{Mark 1:30-34; § 43}

Simon's mother-in-law was in bed with a fever, and they told Jesus about her. So he went to her, took her hand and helped her up. The fever left her and she began to wait on them. That evening after sunset the people brought to Jesus all the sick and demon-possessed. The whole town gathered at the door, and Jesus healed many who had various diseases. He also drove out many demons, but he would not let the demons speak because they knew who he was.

After the circus in the synagogue, Peter and Co. made their way home. They arrived late and hungry. Even so, lunch was not quite ready. Why? Because Peter's mother-in-law was sick in bed and Mrs. Peter had to work it alone. That's okay. Jesus tends to be patient with these sorts of things. However, while they were waiting, instead of immersing themselves in the football game, Peter presents her problem to Jesus. You know how it is when you have a doctor in the house. Jesus is there, why not have a look at the patient?!

She had a dangerously high fever for a woman of her age. Jesus stands by her bedside and takes hold of her hand. Instantly she feels this flush run through her body. Her strength returns and fills her frame. She is healed so thoroughly that she gets up and waits on them over a meal. Jesus not only conquered the sickness, he eradicated the aftermath of fatigue from the fever. That's impressive! More impressive still is the way Jesus healed her. There were no cold compresses, no aspirin, no shaman's dances. He simply rebuked the fever. That's right, he talked to it. He ordered it around as if it were an animate object, and it went away. The astute reader will remember that this is exactly how Jesus exorcized the demoniac. In fact, the same word is used in both Luke 4:35 and 39 (*epetimēsen*). Luke seems to be purposefully showing the connection between these two episodes. Jesus rebukes both demons and sickness — both are treated as works of the devil. When he ushers in the kingdom of God, the works of the devil begin to unravel.

All this took place on the Sabbath. Most people were nestled in their homes. Yet somehow the news of this healing leaked out. Like pollen in spring, it wafted across this small community. By the time the Sabbath ended at sunset, the flurry of activity began. All in Capernaum who were sick and diseased, possessed and dispossessed, began streaming to Peter's door. One can only imagine the scene. Jesus wades his way through humanity, stopping with each individual long enough to hear their story, feel their pain, and eradicate their suffering. Each victim was transformed into a victor. Each raised a shout of praise. Tears of agony were replaced with tears of joy. Families embraced, children danced, and God smiled. And in the middle of it all stood Jesus, his head thrown back in a full throttle belly laugh. Like ripples from a pebble thrown in a pond, the celebration followed Jesus through the crowd. Everyone came with their sick; none were turned away. The jubilation lasted till the early morning hours when the last patient was finally healed. The gates of hell were accosted that day by the kingdom of God — and they crumbled under the weight of Divine love. As the last family made their way home hand in hand, Jesus turned around and looked up an empty street strewn with bloodied bandages, weathered crutches, and empty cots. There he must have smiled a knowing smile, for this was just the beginning.

One might suggest that such episodes are only peripheral to Jesus' true ministry. The real deal is the cross, you know. Yet one must be wary of too small a view of Jesus. Hear what Matthew says. He cites Isaiah 53:4, that marvelous Messianic text on redemption, "He took up our infirmities and carried our diseases." Oh sure, Peter applies this very text to the work of the cross (1 Pet. 2:24). For sure, it includes the eradication of our sins. But Matthew is just as inspired, and he applies it to Jesus' healing our physical diseases. Jesus' ministry *does* target our bodies as well as our souls. Surely this must sound strange against the backdrop of a disease-ridden world. Surely this seems odd in light of the fact that all these folks Jesus healed eventually died. But again, we must guard against a shortsighted view of Jesus. His healing *is* at the cross! And it *does* include our physical bodies. But his cross-work is not yet finished. When he redeems this world at his Second Coming, there will be new bodies in store for us. You see, this scene is not a prediction of A.D. 33 to 2000+. Rather, it is a picture of his glorious return when even the physical creation will be restored to its natural state. Someday, all doctors will be as irrelevant as preachers. Bandages and crutches will go the way of jail cells and prisons. Then, at last, the work of the cross will be complete. Until then, know this, it is too small a thing for Jesus to purchase your soul. He wants to redeem your physical body as well. Soon and very soon you will see this with your own eyes.

Further Reading: Psalm 23; Luke 23:35.

Ponderable Questions: If Jesus had his way and Satan was out of the way, how do you think your life would look? When was the last time you were really sick? How did Jesus show himself kind during that situation? How is this text a preview of heaven? What does it have to do with the cross?

Considerations for Prayer: Thank God for all the ways he's brought healing into your life.

His Problem Was More than Skin Deep

{Luke 5:12-14; § 45}

While Jesus was in one of the towns, a man came along who was covered with leprosy. When he saw Jesus, he fell with his face to the ground and begged him, "Lord, if you are willing, you can make me clean." Jesus reached out his hand and touched the man. "I am willing," he said. "Be clean!" And immediately the leprosy left him. Then Jesus ordered him, "Don't tell anyone, but go, show yourself to the priest and offer the sacrifices that Moses commanded for your cleansing, as a testimony to them."

Leprosy was a horrible disease! Even what we call leprosy today doesn't come close to the biblical descriptions of this peculiar (and probably extinct) condition. For example, Leviticus 13 describes it as a swelling, eruption, a scab, or a bright spot (v. 2). The hair on the sore sometimes turns white, and often the infection visibly spreads beneath the skin (v. 3). It leaves raw sores that ooze with puss or boils that burst (vv. 14,18-20). Often it is attended with baldness, yellow hair on the infected area and a mealy white rash on the face or scalp (vv. 29-31). It was highly infectious. Not only could other people catch it, it could apparently spread to the plaster in the walls of your house, leather products, or even clothing. That's why lepers were kicked out of the village.

In addition to being seriously ill, lepers were also ostracized. In Palestine, being cut off from family and synagogue was horrible business. Worse still, leprosy had a stigma attached to it. People assumed that one got leprosy because of some sin. So expulsion sometimes evolved into open hostility. Not only were they banished from family, they weren't even allowed to engage strangers. The Mosaic Law required lepers to warn passersby that they were infected. They had to shout, "Unclean, unclean." Rabbis in Jesus' day were merciless to leprous "sinners." One rabbi, in fact, boasted that he threw rocks at lepers to keep them away.

Then there was this rabbi named Jesus. One day while walking along the highway a leper spotted him. Against custom and propriety he ran up to Jesus. Instead of crying "unclean" he pleads, "If you are willing, you can make me clean." If you think the Apostles recoiled at Levi, the tax collector, you should have seen them with this human scab. Question: What made this guy think that Jesus was any different than the other rabbis who had abused him? In fact, what made him think that Jesus had the power to help him at all? There is NO precedent to give this man any hope of help. The only two recorded healings of leprosy were Naaman and Miriam. Both were healed by God alone, without direct human intervention.

There is just something about Jesus — something in the way he talks, the way he looks at you — that lets you know he will not turn you away. This is most winsome and extraordinary: to truly be accepted in spite of yourself. Others see the scabs and assume some secret sin. Sometimes we even begin to believe it ourselves. This is a hideous lie from the pits of hell, that there is nothing worthwhile in us, nothing worth loving, nothing worth saving. Only Jesus' piercing presence can dispel this insufferable rumor that we are ugly and untouchable.

Everyone else recoiled in order to protect their own ritual purity. Jesus touched. The audible gasp shot through the apostolic band for fear that Jesus would render himself unclean. Then they gasp again to realize that love incarnate cannot be overcome by uncleanness. This work of the devil encountered the kingdom. It didn't have a prayer to survive.

Satan still renders folks unclean. They're not required to shout "unclean" anymore. But Satan still whispers those same self-condemning words into our souls: "You are dirty. You're refuse. You deserve to be lonely." Jesus still sees beneath the boils to a soul worth saving. If we will but ask, "Are you willing . . ." we'll soon feel the touch that overpowers all uncleanness. Can you not now hear him? "I am willing, be clean!"

Further Reading: Leviticus 13; "Leprosy" — available in electronic form from College Press.

Ponderable Questions: Can you remember a time that you were made to feel dirty? What did you need most during that time to restore you? How can we touch dirty people like Jesus did to bring them healing? What might be some of the ramifications in your church for doing so?

Considerations for Prayer: "Lord, if you are willing, please make me clean." Sit quietly, meditate on the cross, and receive his touch.

Faith of the Four, Forgiveness of the One

{Mark 2:1-12; § 46}

Some men came, bringing to him a paralytic, carried by four of them. Since they could not get him to Jesus because of the crowd, they made an opening in the roof above Jesus and, after digging through it, lowered the mat the paralyzed man was lying on. When Jesus saw their faith, he said to the paralytic, "Son, your sins are forgiven." Now some teachers of the law were sitting there, thinking to themselves, "Why does this fellow talk like that? He's blaspheming! Who can forgive sins but God alone?" . . . "That you may

> know that the Son of Man has authority on earth to forgive sins. . . ." He said to the paralytic, "I tell you, get up, take your mat and go home." He got up, took his mat and walked out in full view of them all.

Who knows how they got in there? Some have suggested they carried his cot up an external stairway. Perhaps a better guess is that these four friends carried their buddy's pallet next door, climbed up the neighbor's roof and carefully walked across a plank balanced between the two homes. From there it was an easy shot down to the awning which shaded Jesus from the sun.

Needless to say, all eyes were not only on Jesus. These faith-filled vandals were a sight to behold. Four men carrying a cot, digging through the awning and lowering their paralyzed partner in front of Jesus, was more than a mild distraction to an otherwise engaging sermon. We'll never know the precise point Jesus was trying to make when this paralytic dropped in. No doubt it was not as striking as the point he is about to make!

"Your sins are forgiven," Jesus declared. Such a statement raised more than a few pharisaic eyebrows. It raised their dander! "Who is this blasphemous braggart who claims God's prerogative?!" The Pharisees may not have the right attitude, or the right faith, but their theology is accurate. Only God can forgive sin. If Jesus can't back up his claim with a miraculous display of power, then he deserves to be punished for overstepping transcendent bounds.

They say it's hard to argue with success. When the lame man walked out, he took with him more than a peasant's pallet. He swept away all doubts that Jesus was God's envoy. Who could argue that Jesus did not have the power to forgive sins when he had the power to make lame men walk? Who would be so bold as to doubt a person of such power? Since you already know the end of the story, I'll not try to keep the Pharisees' plan a secret. They somehow mustered the gall to ignore the miracle and murder Jesus for blasphemy. They believed that he could heal but not that he could forgive sins.

Oddly, this is not so different than many Christians are today. Many of us accept Jesus' healing, but not his forgiveness. Here's what I mean. It seems strange that Christians talk of the wondrous power of Jesus to heal. We sing his praise for he is the king who puts Humpty Dumpties back together again. Many of us give thanks as ex-lame men. To the praise of God, and often with the help of good friends, we stand on our feet again. We often accept his healing but not his forgiveness. Yet he has proven his power to do both. Why do we allow him to put us on our feet, but not let go of the shame that laid us low? How dare we hold on to the guilt that Jesus came to set us free from! He told the lame man, "Get up, take up your pallet and walk." Perhaps his command to you would be, "Rise up. Let go of your baggage and walk."

Further Reading: Romans 8:1-2,31-39.

Ponderable Questions: Why did the Pharisees think it blasphemous for Jesus to offer this man forgiveness of sins? In light of Acts 3:1-11, how do the healings of lame men mirror our own experience of conversion? Is there some sin from your past that you have not let go?

Considerations for Prayer: Confess your past sins to Jesus, then fully release them to his grace.

No Lord! Anybody but *Him*

{Mark 2:13-17; § 47}

> Once again Jesus went out beside the lake. A large crowd came to him, and he began to teach them. As he walked along, he saw Levi son of Alphaeus sitting at the tax collector's booth. "Follow me," Jesus told him, and Levi got up and followed him. While Jesus was having dinner at Levi's house, many tax collectors and "sinners" were eating with him and his disciples, for there were many who followed him. When the teachers of the law who were Pharisees saw him eating with the "sinners" and tax collectors, they asked his disciples: "Why does he eat with tax collectors and 'sinners'?" On hearing this, Jesus said to them, "It is not the healthy who need a doctor, but the sick. I have not come to call the righteous, but sinners."

This is not the first time Jesus asked someone to give up their vocation to follow him. Remember how he called the four fishermen? Matthew's call, however, is more striking. Peter didn't really give up his vocation. He simply surrendered the nets to his family and employees who, no doubt, kept generating revenue for the traveling fishers of men. Whenever he chose, he could return to fishing. Not so with Levi.

He leaves his briefcase at the tax booth next to a long line of loan sharks itching to step into his shoes. When one abandoned the corporate ladder of the Roman IRS, he eliminated any chance of ever returning. Thus, when Levi left, he left everything! He left a lucrative job to follow an itinerant peasant prophet. He left pretentious parties and life in the fast lane. Undoubtedly he left many friends who could hardly understand his passion for Jesus after drinking full from the pagan goblet of hedonism.

So Levi joins this small band of renegades. It was a shock, for sure. These blue collar workers and zealots would hardly take kindly to *him*. As an employee of Rome, he was a Benedict Arnold. It was no picnic for Matthew either, of course. He was used to kudos and sandal licking, not the kind of open aggression that surely shadowed him amidst this apostolic band. Besides, he should have been the treasurer, not Judas!

Indeed, Matthew's sacrifice to follow Jesus is impressive but it gets better. After Jesus' ascension, he takes quill in hand and records his memories of Jesus' ministry. Theologians are especially fond of Matthew's memoirs because they are so full of Old Testament quotations. It piques our curiosity. His book is more than theological novelty, however. He was attempting to penetrate hearts, not merely minds. What makes this so striking is that this Jewish "turncoat" went way back to his roots in an attempt to reach the very people who had ostracized him. The fact is, they had excommunicated him from the synagogue. When everyone else saw a traitor, Jesus saw a teacher. Somehow he delved deep into Matthew's soul. There he found a deep vein of faith. Matthew's sleepless nights, pouring over a Torah scroll in search for the hope of Israel, finally paid off. When he saw Jesus, one word, one invitation was sufficient to capture his soul.

Many modern followers of Jesus share Matthew's story. Maybe you're one of them. Prior to coming to Jesus, perhaps you hid your spiritual longings. You didn't want anyone to know what was really going on inside your heart. You put on the mask of tax collector and sinner. You filled your days with corporate ambition and your nights with fermented celebrations. Your friends were just like you, dangling with trinkets but hollow. You wanted to change but didn't know where to turn. You imagined that one more rung on the ladder of success, one more thrill around the next corner would turn up the meaning of life that heretofore alluded you. Then all of a sudden Jesus met you and with one simple word unmasked you. Bare before the pearl of great price you were at once painfully exposed and comfortably at home. No one else had seen the real you. Jesus did. More than that, he liked what he saw.

In spite of your rebellion, regardless of how you have been ostracized, even by religious people, Jesus wants to encounter you today. He is ready to take you just as you are and make you into what you could never have otherwise become. Can you hear him say, "Come, follow me!"? Whatever you have in your hands or in your Palm Pilot, just lay it down. According to Matthew, it's time for a party!

Further Reading: Matthew 9:9-13; Galatians 1:13-24.

Ponderable Questions: If you're in a group, have each person share their conversion story. Whose is closest to Matthew's? What has it cost you to follow Jesus? What have you gained in the process?

Considerations for Prayer: Pray for someone you know who is like Matthew, who seems so far from the things of God. Ask that s/he would find her/his heart's desire in Jesus.

It's Time for a New Thing

{Luke 5:33-39; § 48}

They said to him, "John's disciples often fast and pray, and so do the disciples of the Pharisees, but yours go on eating and drinking." Jesus answered, "Can you make the guests of the bridegroom fast while he is with them? But the time will come when the bridegroom will be taken from them; in those days they will fast." He told them this parable: "No one tears a patch from a new garment and sews it on an old one. If he does, he will have torn the new garment, and the patch from the new will not match the old. And no one pours new wine into old wineskins. If he does, the new wine will burst the skins, the wine will run out and the wineskins will be ruined. No, new wine must be poured into new wineskins. And no one after drinking old wine wants the new, for he says, 'The old is better.'"

Talk about party poopers! These Pharisees are a bit bent out of shape. They don't take too kindly to Jesus hangin' with Levi and his ilk. You know what they say, "Birds of a feather flock together." This party proved that Jesus was a winebibber and a glutton, not the Messiah some took him for. So they set out surreptitiously to undermine his support base. Get this. Instead of a frontal attack on Jesus, they corner his disciples who are, undoubtedly, already a bit uneasy about Jesus' new friends.

Their sneaky little scheme goes something like this. The Pharisees saunter up to the disciples of John the Baptist. These two groups don't normally get along so well. Yet both agree that Jesus' behavior is inappropriate. So they have some common ground, for the time being. The Pharisees simply ask a question, "Say, why do you suppose that we Pharisees fast, and you Baptists fast, but the Jesus people don't?" You can just hear them, "Hey, that's right. How come they feast while we fast? Shouldn't they be a bit more 'spiritual'? We want a Messiah, not a party animal." Consequently, the Baptists accost the Jesus people, who are already a bit unnerved. Meanwhile, the Pharisees watch from the wings with impish grins as the Baptists parrot their question. The disciples are stymied. Jesus comes to the rescue.

"The friends of the bridegroom don't fast while he is with them!" Jesus says. That would be insulting and inappropriate. It would be as wacky as sewing an unshrunk patch onto an old pair of jeans. As soon as you wash them, both are ruined. It would be as stupid as putting new wine in an old, brittle wineskin. As soon as it ferments, the gasses would burst the skin and both would be lost. The point is simple: To fast now would be inappropriate. Jesus is here and it is time for celebration.

There are a number of lessons that can be drawn from this encounter. But the main point is this: Out with the old and in with new. Jesus replaces the old law and ushers in a new way of living. Oh sure, there will be times of fasting, especially now, as Jesus is physically distanced from us. But by and large, Jesus ushers in celebration. The kingdom of God, which will ultimately culminate in the bridegroom's banquet, even now showers delights on her citizens. This is the age of new wine and festivals. The ascetics among us still try to convince us that those with smiles are somehow spiritually shallow. We feel that we are supposed to be suffering and mourning rather than feasting and dancing. Yet to the extent that the bridegroom is present among us, we celebrate with unmitigated jubilation. Anything less is inappropriate.

Further Reading: 2 Corinthians 5:17; Romans 7:6; 1 Peter 1:3.

Ponderable Questions: In what ways was Christianity "new and improved" from Judaism? Why is it inappropriate for Christians to be sullen? How is the idea that Christians should be ascetics perpetuated in today's church and society at large? How can we balance a life of celebration in Jesus with a serious commitment to prophetic denunciation of evil?

Considerations for Prayer: Ask Jesus to help you balance a prophet's tears with a bride's giddy laugh. Make a list with God of all the reasons you have to rejoice in the newness of Christianity.

The Ingrate and Infidels

{John 5:1-15; § 49}

Now there is in Jerusalem near the Sheep Gate a pool, which in Aramaic is called Bethesda and which is surrounded by five covered colonnades. Here a great number of disabled people used to lie—the blind, the lame, the paralyzed. One who was there had been an invalid for thirty-eight years. When Jesus saw him lying there and learned that he had been in this condition for a long time, he asked him, "Do you want to get well?" "Sir," the invalid replied, "I have no one to help me into the pool when the water is stirred. While I am trying to get in, someone else goes down ahead of me." Then Jesus said to him, "Get up! Pick up your mat and walk." At once the man was cured; he picked up his mat and walked. The day on which this took place was a Sabbath . . . . Later Jesus found him at the temple and said to him, "See, you are well again. Stop sinning or something worse may happen to you." The man went away and told the Jews that it was Jesus who had made him well.

I don't like this guy . . . not even a little bit. It is probably not politically correct to pick on a cripple, but when he lacks both faith and courage what can you do? He sits all day by the pool of Bethesda waiting for the waters to stir. He has bought into the local lore that suggests the first person into the bubbling pool gets healed by God. Now isn't that a pretty pickle? The person who needs healing the least is the one who gets it! No doubt, that was the superstition in vogue. However, there are serious doubts as to whether God operates that way. The Bible doesn't say God helps those who help themselves. Rather, it suggests that God helps the helpless.

Back to our boy. He sits there steeped in superstition. Worse yet, he has no one to help him in the pool. That's not necessarily his fault. However, when Jesus comes along and offers him help, all he does is complain about being helpless. Jesus orders him up and out of the sick ward. Off he goes, carrying his cot as directed. But wait . . . it was a Sabbath day . . . storm clouds are brewing.

Off he scampers to the temple. You realize, of course, that this would be the first time in thirty-eight years (perhaps in all his life) he was able to enter the temple. Problem: He is carrying his cot on the Sabbath day. He is accosted by the Jewish leaders. They are appalled at this plebeian flaunting their oral laws. In his own defense he passes the buck to Jesus. "The man who healed me told me to do it," he said. The leaders, of course, wanted a name. This poor fellow had no idea who Jesus was. All this left him feeling a bit sheepish and spanked on a day that should have been the happiest of his life. It will get worse.

A little while later Jesus catches up with this man in the temple. He adds his own rebuke to the charges leveled by the Jewish leaders. "Stop sinning," he said, "or something worse will happen to you." Yikes! The man, by now, must be quivering in his tunic. This ex-cripple runs off and finks on Jesus. The Pharisees move in like buzzards on carrion. Let the games begin! This is a knock-down-drag-out of colossal proportions.

They ask Jesus why he would order a man, against tradition, to take up his pallet and walk. This is an important question. In fact, the next two sections will deal with this very issue of breaking the Sabbath regulations. Normally such Sabbath controversies end with Jesus telling his opponents how important people are. Here, however, he tells them how important HE is. This sermon in John 5:19-47 is a striking declaration of Jesus' deity and credentials. He is one with the Father and one who raises the dead. He is the judge of the whole world and arbiter of eternal destinies. These claims infuriate Jesus' antagonists. In fact, from that point on, they redoubled their efforts to kill him (v. 18).

Jesus was not just a do-gooder. He was not simply a clever teacher. His words and deeds, wedded together in this text, demand that we come to some conclusion about him. We can't like what he does but not listen to what he says. We dare not follow him out of curiosity without submission to his authority. We must not "damn him with faint praise," saying such vapid and shallow things as "He was a good man but not the Son of God." No, either we love him and serve him, or we deny and assassinate him. When you are sandwiched between the deeds of Jesus (vv. 1-8) and his claims (vv. 19-45), there is simply no middle ground for casual devotees.

Further Reading: John 5:1-47; "Sermon on Deity" — available in electronic form from College Press.

Ponderable Questions: What claims does Jesus make about himself in this sermon? Walk through the list of claims considering (1) how Jesus substantiated each and (2) what demands each make on my life. What are some of the reasons this paralytic at the pool might have had such a hard time believing in Jesus?

Considerations for Prayer: Use this list of claims as a foundation for praise.

---

18 Picking on the Sabbath 18

{Matthew 12:1-8; § 50}

At that time Jesus went through the grainfields on the Sabbath. His disciples were hungry and began to pick some heads of grain and eat them. When the Pharisees saw this, they said to him, "Look! Your disciples are doing what is unlawful on the Sabbath." He answered, "Haven't you read what David did when he and his companions were hungry? He entered the house of God, and he and his companions ate the consecrated bread—which was not lawful for them to do, but only for the priests. Or haven't you read in the Law that on the Sabbath the priests in the temple desecrate the day and yet are innocent? I tell you that one greater than the temple is here. If you had known what these words mean, 'I desire mercy, not sacrifice,' you would not have condemned the innocent. For the Son of Man is Lord of the Sabbath."

Jesus and his band of merry men were strolling through the grainfields mid-harvest. They got hungry. Naturally, they grabbed a few heads of grain from the edges of the field for an afternoon snack. That was perfectly permissible. In Jewish law the corners of the fields were reserved for the poor and for pilgrims. Even so the Pharisees flinch. Why? Not because the disciples were stealing, but because they were "working" on the Sabbath. That's right. The Jewish oral traditions specifically said that to pick grain is to reap, to roll it in your hands is to thresh, and to blow the chaff off your palms is to winnow. Talk about persnickety! Nonetheless, the traditions were clearly on the side of the opposition.

They demanded that Jesus explain the behavior of his disciples. He responds with two very unusual illustrations. First, David, against the written law, ate the shewbread and gave some to his men. What's worse, he did it when he was running away from the king and after lying to the High Priest about his mission. Nevertheless David was never charged with wrongdoing. Second, the priests slaughter animals for sacrifice every Sabbath with immunity. They carry out deliberate and bloody work without desecrating the holy day. How? Precisely because they are fulfilling the obligations of temple worship.

Now, what do these two examples prove? Two things according to Jesus. First, he says, "I tell you that one greater than the temple is here" (v. 6). This is classic Jewish logic from the least to the greatest. David could break the law with immunity, so could the priests of the temple. Here stands the fulfillment of both David and the temple. Obviously Jesus and his disciples have certain immunities because of their higher status than even David and the temple. Furthermore, because he is Lord of the Sabbath (v. 8), he gets to set the rules. Needless to say, the Pharisees would have choked on that one! Yet this argument is imperative for Christian theology. Jesus is the fulfillment of all the major hopes and dreams of Israel. He is our temple, our king, our holy mountain, our river of living water, our Torah, our Moses, even our promised land. This text is not recorded so that we can marvel at Jesus' logic. Rather, it is recorded so we can celebrate his person!

Second, Jesus argues from Hosea 6:6 that mercy is greater than sacrifice. Or as Mark records the incident: "The Sabbath was made for man, not man for the Sabbath" (Mark 2:27). In other words, human needs always supersede the law. If David's need superseded the written law of God, it is no small wonder that the disciples' need superseded the oral law of the Pharisees. One might argue that the disciples' need could hardly be compared to the life threat that David and his company faced. True, but Jesus would respond that the same heart of compassion that acquits David would also absolve the disciples. When we follow Jesus, the Lord of the Sabbath, we tend to interpret God's laws through shades of compassion rather than obligation. When we follow the merciful master, we tend to see God's provisions for people rather than his demands of them.

Further Reading: Hebrews 4:1-11, "Sabbath" and "Messianic Expectations" — available in electronic form from College Press.

Ponderable Questions: What kind of "Sabbath regulations" do we have in our churches? In other words, what are our own sacred cows which are not founded on Scripture? In what ways might these sometimes supersede compassion? Jesus fulfilled the Sabbath, the temple, and Davidic kingship. What other Jewish hopes and dreams did he fulfill?

Considerations for Prayer: Ask God to help you see yourself and your church through the lens of his priorities. Plead with God to help you find Sabbath in Jesus — to rest in him.

---

19 Give Him a Hand 19

{Mark 3:1-6; § 51}

Another time he went into the synagogue, and a man with a shriveled hand was there. Some of them were looking for a reason to accuse Jesus, so they watched him closely to see if he would heal him on the Sabbath. Jesus said to the man with the shriveled hand, "Stand up in front of everyone." Then Jesus asked them, "Which is lawful on the Sabbath: to do good or to do evil, to save life or to kill?" But they remained silent. He looked around at them in anger and, deeply distressed at their stubborn hearts, said to the man, "Stretch out your hand." He stretched it out, and his hand was completely restored. Then the Pharisees went out and began to plot with the Herodians how they might kill Jesus.

Jesus is quickly gaining a reputation for disregarding the traditional rules of the Sabbath. The Pharisees are getting more than mildly miffed. So they lay in wait at the local synagogue, watching for a sufficient cause to kill him. They won't have to wait long.

There is a man there whose hand was shriveled. One early church father named Jerome suggested that he had been a mason and was injured in an accident. Regardless, he had few vocational options open to him in Palestine. He is in dire straits. Undoubtedly, he longs for healing, but surely he doesn't crave the publicity that this particular healing affords. No one really likes having their handicap highlighted.

Jesus knows the Pharisees' motives. He calls the man front and center. Peering at the religious leaders, he asks, "Is it lawful to do good on the Sabbath or evil? To save a life or kill?" The answer is so obvious! Yet they remain silent. Had they responded, they surely would have said, "Jesus, you are asking two different questions. We are not suggesting you do evil on the Sabbath, only that you refrain from healing until sunset. Furthermore, waiting a few hours to heal this man is NOT going to kill him!" Yet for Jesus, to refrain from good when it is in one's power is tantamount to doing evil. To withhold healing, even for the sake of Sabbath, is equivalent to killing.

Their silence is deafening. Jesus' anger is visible. That should get our attention. After all, it is not a good idea to enrage the one who can quiet storms! More striking still is the fact that Jesus seldom gets angry. In fact, there are only three times his wrath is recorded: Here, at the cleansing of the temple, and when the disciples refused to allow the children access to Jesus. On all three occasions, religious men (the Pharisees [Mark 3:1-6], Sadducees [John 2:13-17], and the Apostles [Matt. 19:13-14], respectively), pushed aside human need in the face of religious ritual. This is what piqued Jesus. He could deal with sinners. It's religious bigots he had such a hard time with.

Further Reading: John 2:13-17; Matthew 19:13-14.

Ponderable Questions: What are the similarities between those three occasions when Jesus got angry? Is there anything in your life that would give him reason to be angry with you? How and for what should we appropriately express Christian anger?

Considerations for Prayer: Repent for the times and ways you have prioritized ritual over people, for times you cared more about law than about mercy.

What Could Possibly Surprise Jesus?

{Luke 7:1-10; § 55}

The centurion heard of Jesus and sent some elders of the Jews to him, asking him to come and heal his servant. When they came to Jesus, they pleaded earnestly with him, "This man deserves to have you do this, because he loves our nation and has built our synagogue." So Jesus went with them. He was not far from the house when the centurion sent friends to say to him: "Lord, don't trouble yourself, for I do not deserve to have you come under my roof. That is why I did not even consider myself worthy to come to you. But say the word, and my servant will be healed. . . ." When Jesus heard this, he was amazed at him, and turning to the crowd following him, he said, "I tell you, I have not found such great faith even in Israel."

Had he been an American soldier rather than a Roman, he would have been called a captain. Back then, however, they were known as centurions — a leader of 100 men. That puts him in an elite circle. Centurions are only mentioned five times in the Bible (Matt. 27:54; Acts 10; 22; 27, and here). Every one of these Roman envoys is painted in glowing colors. Thus, we already suspect he will wear a white hat in this text.

He had come to Palestine as part of the extensive Roman peace-keeping forces. Normally they were not well liked. But this man was different. He had contributed much to his new community. In fact, he built the Jewish synagogue, and they loved him for it. The text doesn't say, but likely he loved these Jews as well. Perhaps his fledgling faith in Yahweh prompted his generosity to the Jewish community.

So, when his servant fell sick, the Jews joined in his mourning. He loved that young man dearly. In fact, Luke uses a word in verse 7 that mean's "child" — he had practically adopted the boy. As the young man drew nearer death's door, something had to be done. Someone remembered this itinerant healer whose headquarters were there in Capernaum. Stories about him were slung across the city's streets. Perhaps the nobleman (John 4), who undoubtedly had dealings with the centurion at Capernaum, even reported a healing of his own servant. It was an amazing miracle that Jesus performed from Cana, some 20 miles away.

A Jewish delegation goes to Jesus on behalf of their synagogue's patron. Jesus agrees to see his patient. As the entourage draws near, however, the centurion sends servants to stop them in their tracks. He knew well the ramifications of a Jewish leader entering the home of a Gentile, particularly a Roman soldier. Jesus is apparently willing to bear the brunt of racist aggression. Nevertheless, the centurion recognizes that this could all be averted. After all, he can order soldiers to come and go as he chooses. Surely Jesus could do the same thing with the spiritual entities at play behind this physical veil of sickness. Jesus stops short in his tracks, both literally and metaphorically. The Bible says he was "astonished." That, in itself, is astonishing. After all, there are only two times that Jesus is amazed. Here he is amazed at the faith of a Gentile. In Mark 6:6 he is amazed at the unbelief of his hometown synagogue.

Now isn't that amazing! Those who should believe won't; those who have no business believing do . . . and in a big way. Question: Do you want to amaze Jesus? If so, you will have a difficult time. No artist can compete with a simple sunrise. No orator can compare with the living Logos. No athlete can walk on water. No magician can raise the dead. If you truly want to amaze Jesus, the only vehicle available is raw, unmitigated faith.

Further Reading: James 2:14-26.

Ponderable Questions: Are you, like the centurion, known as a person of faith? What expressions of faith do you think Jesus would commend you for today? Where would he want to stretch you? Is there a danger in being too gullible and calling it faith?

Considerations for Prayer: Pray that your faith would be evident today in your actions, not so that your words become unnecessary, but so they would become believable.

An Heir Raising Experience

{Luke 7:11-16; § 56}

Soon afterward, Jesus went to a town called Nain, and his disciples and a large crowd went along with him. As he approached the town gate, a dead person was being carried out—the only son of his mother, and she was a widow. And a large crowd from the town was with her. When the Lord saw her, his heart went out to her and he said, "Don't cry." Then he went up and touched the coffin, and those carrying it stood still. He said, "Young man, I say to you, get up!" The dead man sat up and began to talk, and Jesus gave him back to his mother. They were all filled with awe and praised God. "A great prophet has appeared among us," they said. "God has come to help his people."

As Jesus' popularity increases, so does his entourage. He travels the 20 miles from Capernaum to Nain with a substantial swarm of followers. As they approach the village gate, they encounter another group trying to get out. Suddenly we have an ancient traffic jam. This was a problem. The crowd coming out of the city was a funeral procession that Jesus inadvertently stopped in its tracks.

Jesus led his procession; a widow led the other. She had already lost her husband and just now lost her son. It is all so sad, more so when one realizes this son was her only social security. Jesus, never untouched by a funeral, feels compassion for her. He wants to help, but his words surely don't. He says to the weeping widow, "Stop crying"! Now that's a fine "how-do-you-do." You can't blame her if she is a little confused by all this. Then Jesus does something that under normal circumstances would be downright rude. He walks over to the coffin and touches it.

Right about now her mind is racing, her stomach turning, and I wouldn't be surprised if her fist didn't clench. But then (if she thinks this is strange, she ain't seen nothin'!), wonder of all wonders, the boy sits up and speaks. The Bible doesn't record what he says, but one thing is certain, he had everyone's undivided attention!

The crowd's reaction is about what you would expect. They were dumbfounded. They praised God. Undoubtedly they broke into laughter, tears, even a bit of dancing. They cried out, "A great prophet has appeared to us. God has come to help his people." Indeed, he had. You might recall that Elijah healed the widow's son at Zarephath (1 Kgs. 17:17-24). His protégée, Elisha, healed the Shunammite woman's son (2 Kgs. 4:32-37). (By the way, Shunem is just over the next hill from Nain. This story struck close to home.) Luke has already paired these two great prophets in Jesus' sermon in Nazareth (4:25-27). In other words, this story is not merely about a wondrous deed that Jesus performed. It is a deliberate comparison by Luke between the power of Jesus and the power of the great prophets Elijah and Elisha.

The conclusion of the crowd is not, "Wow! What a great gig." Rather it is, "God has visited us." The miracle was only a prelude to the person. Jesus is clearly God's envoy. That means salvation is near; the divine cavalry has come. Yet that cavalry would meet Calvary. This boy too would someday face death again. Does this mean God failed? No, of course not. The story doesn't end at the grave. These are merely previews of things to come. As glorious as this boy's resuscitation was, it pales in comparison to the resurrection it promises. Through the tears that shroud this veil of death, this little tale of an unnamed widow's son reminds us of better things to come.

Further Reading: John 5:24-29; 1 Thessalonians 4:13-17.

Ponderable Questions: What are the theological implications of Jesus' reenacting Elijah's miracle? How do you think you would have responded had you witnessed this miracle? Would this radical miracle be any more easily believed back then than it is today? What do you think your own resurrection will be like, both the experience and your body?

Considerations for Prayer: Bless the name of the Lord, whose power extends even over death.

True Greatness

{Luke 7:20-28; § 57}

When the men came to Jesus, they said, "John the Baptist sent us to you to ask, 'Are you the one who was to come, or should we expect someone else?'" At that very time Jesus cured many who had diseases, sicknesses and evil spirits, and gave sight to many who were blind. So he replied to the messengers, "Go back and report to John what you have seen and heard: The blind receive sight, the lame walk, those who have leprosy are cured, the deaf hear, the dead are raised, and the good news is preached to the poor. Blessed is the man who does not fall away on account of me." After John's messengers left, Jesus began to speak to the crowd about John: "What did you go out into the desert to see?. . . A prophet? Yes, I tell you, and more than a prophet. . . . I tell you, among those born of women there is no one greater than John; yet the one who is least in the kingdom of God is greater than he."

My own doubts and limited faith seldom shock me. But when my mentors and heroes question the kingdom, that shakes me up a bit. This is why John's question is so disturbing. Granted, he has been in prison for ten months with no Messianic rescue. Furthermore, Jesus looks a lot different than John and carries out his ministry as a socialite rather than an ascetic. So John's doubts are not unfounded, just unexpected. One can only imagine how the disciples felt to hear such misgivings from a man that many of them had also called Rabbi.

Jesus' response is reasonable. At that very time Jesus was engaged in an extensive healing campaign. It included the eradication of various diseases, the exorcism of demons, cleansing of leprosy, raising paralytics, giving sight to the blind, and even raising the dead. Best of all, he preached the good news to the poor. These alone should be sufficient to eradicate all doubt from John's mind.

As John's two envoys turn on their heels to return to their mentor, Jesus sings his praise. "John," he says, "was no wimpy reed blown by the winds of current popularity. Nor was he some pampered pansy from a palace." What was he then? A prophet! Not just any prophet, but the forerunner of the Messiah as predicted in Malachi 3:1. His role as Jesus' precursor didn't just put him in elite company, it propelled him ahead of the pack. Jesus said, "Among those born of women there is no one greater than John." What a statement! This miracleless meanderer was greater than Moses. This childless ascetic was more important than Abraham, more prominent than the prophets, more revered than David. Is that possibly true? Yes, but only because of his relationship with Jesus. The job of introducing Jesus was given to John. This responsibility was his privilege, and his privilege was his prominence.

If you think this is astounding, wait till you hear the second half of Jesus' statement: "Yet the one who is least in the kingdom of God is greater than he." *No way!* "Do you mean that the grungiest Christian is greater than John?" Yes! But only because of our relationship with Jesus. You see, John could only announce Jesus' *coming*. We can announce his *deliverance*. He spoke of Jesus' appearance, we speak of his resurrection. He called for repentance, we promise forgiveness. Above and beyond all this we have what none of the prophets and fathers had — the Holy Spirit of God. This Spirit brings us into a dynamic relationship with the Lord that supersedes all that came before us. Are you eager to fellowship with Moses and Elijah? Do you have some questions for Noah and Abraham? Do you long to worship with David or quiz Solomon? Listen, they are far more interested in your experience than you could possibly be in theirs. This is truly astounding! Your life, because of the Spirit of Christ, is far greater than theirs.

Further Reading: Hebrews 11:39-40; "John's Testimony about Jesus" — available in electronic form from College Press.

Ponderable Questions: Recount a time when a mentor of yours expressed doubt or showed vulnerability. What did that do to you? Enumerate the reasons why Christians are greater than the O.T. saints. How does this list affect your self-image and your zeal to serve Christ?

Considerations for Prayer: Beseech God for the Holy Spirit to empower you to live up to all he has invested in you.

23 Clean Feet, Clean Soul 23

{Luke 7:37-39,47b-50; § 59}

When a woman who had lived a sinful life in that town learned that Jesus was eating at the Pharisee's house, she brought an alabaster jar of perfume, and as she stood behind him at his feet weeping, she began to wet his feet with her tears. Then she wiped them with her hair, kissed them and poured perfume on them. When the Pharisee who had invited him saw this, he said to himself, "If this man were a prophet, he would know who is touching him and what kind of woman she is—that she is a sinner." . . . "I tell you, her many sins have been forgiven—for she loved much. But he who has been forgiven little loves little." Then Jesus said to her, "Your sins are forgiven." The other guests began to say among themselves, "Who is this who even forgives sins?" Jesus said to the woman, "Your faith has saved you; go in peace."

Meals in Palestine were not merely social, they were often political. In Luke's writings they are not merely physical, they are invariably spiritual. As this story unfolds, all that happens with the Pharisee will be politically charged at the table while all that happens with the woman will be spiritually rich. There's food for thought here.

Simon invites Jesus to join him for supper. It is a special banquet inundated with power and pomp. Everybody who was anybody was reclined around the table. Theology and politics were bantered about as wise men and power brokers jostled for rank. Jesus is the center of attention and strangely disinterested in it all.

From stage left enters a woman. Her mere presence silences the aristocrats. In consternation they watch as this common whore approaches Jesus. He is sprawled out on elegant cushions beside Simon his host (who is, no doubt, now approaching a fetal position, recoiling from this wanton woman). She says nothing. Tears fall in waves over Jesus' dusty feet. Without explanation, she kneels to wipe the now muddied feet with her hair. Taking them in her hands, she kisses them. She rubs them with ointment from a translucent stone jar slung around her neck. She kisses them some more. The woman is obviously broken. Simon is obviously appalled. Jesus is simply Jesus.

"Simon," Jesus asked, "Who would love a loan shark more? The one forgiven of a $50,000 debt, or one released from $2,000?" "That's simple," Simon says, "The greater the debt, the greater the love." "Yes," Jesus replies, "That's why she loves me more than you do." Simon had neglected the conventional kiss and foot washing. He ignored the anointing due such dignitaries. In contrast, this woman exploded convention with lavish worship.

Jesus now explodes their conventional theology by declaring her sins forgiven. This triggers a tremor throughout the banquet hall. Simon's associates know their Bible well — this is blasphemy. They whisper in angry tones, "Only God can forgive sins." This hearkens back to the paralytic (Mark 2:1-12). This is the very debate Jesus won earlier. Yet behind this winnable argument, Jesus sees a broken soul. The argument drops by the wayside; the woman is placed front and center. Still kissing his feet, she looks in his eyes and hears him say these words, "Your faith has saved you; go in peace."

Her silent worship attests to faith much louder than shouts of praise. Yet strange is Jesus' benediction. How can he say to her, "Go in peace"? If she follows the way of Jesus, she leaves unemployed — penniless, jobless, friendless. She leaves her valued ointment with Jesus, yet her reputation is still intact. For all intents and purposes, she leaves the room worse than when she arrived, save this one thing: She is forgiven. This, amidst life's greatest loss and pain, is sufficient for the Master to say, "Go in peace." Still today, for those who wash his feet with tears, he turns about and cleanses their soul. If you have sufficient faith, and perhaps a bit of ointment, you too can walk out with this woman, liberated from a painful past, resilient in the face of a difficult present. For forgiveness is clearly more powerful than both.

Further Reading: 1 John 1:8-10.

Ponderable Questions: Jesus said those who have been forgiven much love much. How have you seen this truth played out? Are you closer to the man in the parable who was forgiven 500 denarii or the one forgiven of 50? How have you been taking Jesus for granted? Does this reflect your awareness of his forgiveness of your debt?

Considerations for Prayer: Confess your sins to God and thank him for canceling your debt.

Brothers and Blasphemy

{Mark 3:21-24,29,31-35; § 61 & 63}

When his family heard about this, they went to take charge of him, for they said, "He is out of his mind." And the teachers of the law who came down from Jerusalem said, "He is possessed by Beelzebub! By the prince of demons he is driving out demons." So Jesus called them and spoke to them in parables: "How can Satan drive out Satan? If a kingdom is divided against itself, that kingdom cannot stand. . . . But whoever blasphemes against the Holy Spirit will never be forgiven; he is guilty of an eternal sin." . . . Then Jesus' mother and brothers arrived. Standing outside, they sent someone in to call him. A crowd was sitting around him, and they told him, "Your mother and brothers are outside looking for you." "Who are my mother and my brothers?" he asked. Then he looked at those seated in a circle around him and said, "Here are my mother and my brothers! Whoever does God's will is my brother and sister and mother."

Mark is fond of sandwiches. He likes to tell stories in such a way that two "outside" events are explained by an incident they surround. In other words, the bread is flavored by the meat. Such is the case with Mark 3:20-35. On either end of this pericope we find Jesus' family trying to get at him. On the front side, they want to take charge of him. (The word is sometimes translated "to capture" or "arrest.") They are convinced that there is something seriously wrong with Jesus. Let's face it, he did have a messiah complex. He is running all around Galilee trying to save everyone. He doesn't even take time to eat (v. 20)! It is ridiculous. You can just hear his brothers say, "If he won't take care of himself, then we'll have to take charge of him." Besides, Jesus was not merely endangering himself, he was embarrassing the family. Claiming to be sent from God! Really! "He is out of his mind," they say.

What's worse, he is the eldest son. Joseph is apparently now dead. Jesus should be caring for the family. He is letting his siblings down. No wonder they come and want a word with him (v. 31). When Jesus is informed that they are waiting outside, he waves them off. You must understand how offensive this would be. The Jewish social world revolved around family loyalty. Jesus has abandoned his birth family and is claiming to have a new fictive family — a made-up group of kin based not on blood but loyalty to the Word of God. This will not sit well at the next family reunion!

That's the bread, now here's the meat. Jesus heals a demoniac who was both blind and mute. This is like Helen Keller meeting Sybil. This man was a mess! Jesus performs this beautiful healing. The crowds are in awe. The Pharisees object. "He does this by the power of the Devil," they say, "not by the power of the Holy Spirit." Boy are they ever wrong! In fact, they wind up calling the Holy Spirit the unholy spirit. That's not just a blunder; that's blasphemy, blasphemy of the unforgivable sort. Now, it is not that the Holy Spirit has real tender feelings and gets irreversibly irate when someone slanders him. It is simply this: God has provided a series of proofs to convince people that Jesus really is the Christ. He gave the Bible, miracles, preaching, signs, etc. There's a lot of evidence marshaled in Jesus' favor. Yet there is still one more, but only one more. The last stop on this series of apologetic proofs was the Holy Spirit. If they missed Him, the abyss below was the only thing left to catch their fall.

How, then, does this meat flavor the bread? The Pharisees were the epitome of Jesus' enemies. The blasphemy of the Holy Spirit is the worst sin they could have committed. Yet Jesus' own family was placed right beside them as if to say, "Look at that! Jesus' brothers acted the same as his enemies." What does this have to do with us? Many try to get to Jesus through the back door. We claim all kinds of "family connections." Perhaps we have been raised in a religious home or we go to the "right" church. Maybe we even have a heritage in the Jesus movement. Jesus rejects all these familial relationships. The only way to have an encounter with Christ is through real, live, bona fide faith. It is only by hearing and obeying the word of God that we can claim to be related to Jesus.

Further Reading: Romans 2:25-29.

Ponderable Questions: What is the blasphemy of the Holy Spirit? How do we, in the church, sometimes act like Jesus' enemies did? In what ways do we sometimes try to connect ourselves with Jesus without faith or commitment to his word? How does Romans 2:25-29 relate to this text?

Considerations for Prayer: Express to the Lord your faith in him and him alone — apart from family, tradition, goodness, or pedigree.

Who Is He Really?

{Mark 4:37-41; § 65}

A furious squall came up, and the waves broke over the boat, so that it was nearly swamped. Jesus was in the stern, sleeping on a cushion. The disciples woke him and said to him, "Teacher, don't you care if we drown?" He got up, rebuked the wind and said to the waves, "Quiet! Be still!" Then the wind died down and it was completely calm. He said to his disciples, "Why are you so afraid? Do you still have no faith?" They were terrified and asked each other, "Who is this? Even the wind and the waves obey him!"

The crowds were oppressively eager to meet Jesus. Everyone wanted to touch him. That's understandable. But he wants to preach. You can imagine the problems created by this conflict of interests. It got so bad one day that Jesus stood in a boat off the shore of Capernaum just so he could preach (Matt.13:1-2). They can hear him, but can't maul him. The subject of the day is the Kingdom of God. He tackles this topic simply by telling stories — parables, they were called — one right after another. Each one got more confusing than the last. By sunset everyone was pretty confused but still as ravenously curious as ever.

It is getting time to bed down for the night. One look at the crowds, however, convinces Jesus that there will be no rest for the weary in Capernaum. So he directs the disciples to start rowing backwards. As they head across the lake, several boats follow, until they are driven back by this storm. It came out of nowhere, as storms often do on the Sea of Galilee.

By this time Jesus is asleep in the back of the boat. Tossed and soaked, he sleeps through it all. The disciples wake him up. "Teacher, don't you care if we drown?" It may look like they want him to save them miraculously, but their response in a moment betrays their little faith. They have no clue what Jesus is able to do, they simply want him to help bail out the boat.

Jesus stands up (a rather foolish move under such circumstances . . . of course, when you can walk on water that greatly reduces the danger). He speaks to the wind and the waves (an equally foolish thing to do). Lo and behold, they listen! The storm is silenced; the disciples stymied.

Jesus turns to them and asks, "Why are you so afraid? Do you still have no faith?" Now wait a minute! No faith?! How much can Jesus expect from these guys. Yes, they have seen him turn water to wine, but that is a mere sleight of hand trick compared to this. Yes, they have seen him heal diseases and demon possession. But these miracles only indicate that he has great spiritual power over the dark forces that cause such sickness. This miracle demonstrates power over the great inanimate forces of nature. Suddenly, they realize he isn't just a great guru, he is the Son of God. Jesus is disappointed they didn't get it before. Strange indeed, they have traveled with him for over a year now, and they haven't a clue as to who Jesus really is until now.

Many of us are in the same boat. We have walked with Jesus for years. He still looks at us as we traverse storms and asks, "Have you no faith?" We confess with our lips that he is the God-man. But most of us act like he isn't even a very good magician. We have difficulty believing that he can handle our money, or children, or schedules. Why is it we believe so little about Jesus? Why is it that when the storm subsides, with mouths agape we say, "I didn't know he could do that"? Why indeed! It's because we lack faith. And, that is really all Jesus asks of us. He is saddened we have so little.

Further Reading: 1 John 5:10-15.

Ponderable Questions: Define faith. Give some examples of how we perpetually doubt Jesus' power even after he has demonstrated his ability to care for us. Why do we have such a difficult time trusting in Jesus? What can we do to increase our faith?

Considerations for Prayer: Ask God to grant you the gift of faith (1 Cor. 12:9).

Deviled Ham

26

{Mark 5:1-3,7-8,11-13a,17-20; § 66}

They went across the lake to the region of the Gerasenes. When Jesus got out of the boat, a man with an evil spirit came from the tombs to meet him. This man lived in the tombs, and no one could bind him any more, not even with a chain. . . . He shouted at the top of his voice, "What do you want with me, Jesus, Son of the Most High God? Swear to God that you won't torture me!" For Jesus had said to him, "Come out of this man, you evil spirit!" . . . A large herd of pigs was feeding on the nearby hillside. The demons begged Jesus, "Send us among the pigs; allow us to go into them." He gave them permission, and the evil spirits came out and went into the pigs. . . . Then the people began to plead with Jesus to leave their region. As Jesus was getting into the boat, the man who had been demon-possessed begged to go with him. Jesus did not let him, but said, "Go home to your family and tell them how much the Lord has done for you, and how he has had mercy on you." So the man went away and began to tell in the Decapolis how much Jesus had done for him.

Usually streakers run away from you; this one would charge you. As Jesus and the disciples land on this Gentile shore of Gerasa they know they're not in Kansas anymore. Bounding down the corpse-filled cliffs comes this deranged demoniac, naked and scarred, unkempt and unclean. He screams at the top of his lungs, "What do you want with me, Jesus, Son of the Most High God? . . ." The disciples, no doubt, step back into the boat and grab the oars. The demoniac comes to a screeching halt at the feet of Jesus. Up on the brow of the cliff are some minimum wage workers tending a herd of pigs. (We'll just call them "sowboys.") They watch with interest as this amazing scene unfolds below.

The legion of demons begs to take up residence in the pigs. Permission is granted. Off they go, both the demons and the pigs. Hog-wild, they race toward the cliff, plummeting to their death. A herd 2,000 strong committed sooeey-cide. The sowboys watching the unholy hogs are in serious trouble. They run into town, wake up the ranchers in the middle of the night, and squeal on Jesus. It doesn't take them too long to round up the posse and return to the scene of the crime. They see the pigs, tails like little flags bobbing up and down in a full moon. They see the demoniac sitting clothed and in his right mind. They see Jesus. He doesn't look so extraordinary, but he has done what neither chain nor magician was able to do.

They encounter the Christ. They must do something with him. Like the demoniac, they can submit to Jesus and sit at his feet. Or like the legion, they can flee from his presence. They choose the latter. Only instead of the farmers leaving, they ask Jesus to (after all, this was their turf). He grants their request and is on his way. This poor ex-demoniac asks to go with him. After all, what kind of future does he have in his hometown? What woman would marry him? What man would give him a job? Jesus, seemingly calloused, says, "No. Go to your friends and family and tell them about me." Undoubtedly sullen, the man watches as his only friend in the world slips off across the lake.

The man did, in fact, do what Jesus commanded. He went home and began to talk about Jesus. One thing led to another, and pretty soon the snowball had reached the entire region. He had become a well-known evangelist in the Decapolis. This is really quite extraordinary on two counts. First, a man with less than six hours of Bible College education evangelizes an entire region. Second, when Jesus returns to the area a second time, instead of being kicked out, he feeds 4,000. Why do the citizens of the Decapolis give Jesus such a different reception the second time around? The Bible doesn't say, but surely it has something to do with a grateful ex-demoniac who couldn't keep his mouth shut. He had no degrees or credentials, simply an encounter with Christ. But that was all he needed to tell his story. Jesus is simply worth talking about.

Further Reading: Matthew 10:32-33; Romans 10:14-15.

Ponderable Questions: Do you know of someone who constantly shares Jesus with others? Testify about the last time you told someone what Jesus did for you. How did they respond? Why do people so seldom talk about Jesus? Is there any way we can present Jesus in simplicity so people will listen?

Considerations for Prayer: Ask God for eyes wide open to opportunities around you and a divine boldness to talk about Jesus' goodness.

Twelve Years and the Trail of Tears

{Mark 5:22-25,28a-29,32-36,40b-41; § 67}

Then one of the synagogue rulers, named Jairus, came there. Seeing Jesus, he fell at his feet and pleaded earnestly with him, "My little daughter is dying. Please come and put your hands on her so that she will be healed and live." So Jesus went with him. A large crowd followed and pressed around him. And a woman was there who had been subject to bleeding for twelve years. . . . She thought, "If I just touch his clothes, I will be healed." Immediately her bleeding stopped and she felt in her body that she was freed from her suffering . . . Jesus kept looking around to see who had done it. Then the woman, knowing what had happened to her, came and fell at his feet and, trembling with fear, told him the whole truth. He said to her, "Daughter, your faith has healed you. Go in peace and be freed from your suffering." While Jesus was still speaking, some men came from the house of Jairus, the synagogue ruler. "Your daughter is dead," they said. "Why bother the teacher any more?" Ignoring what they said, Jesus told the synagogue ruler, "Don't be afraid; just believe." . . . After he put them all out, he took the child's father and mother and the disciples who were with him, and went in where the child was. He took her by the hand and said to her, "Talitha koum!" (which means, "Little girl, I say to you, get up!").

The crowds are so thick they are dangerous. Luke says they "almost crushed him" (Luke 8:42). Everyone wants a piece of Jesus and they are not even polite about it. They push and shove, claw and clamor. Two of them win the day. The first is a synagogue ruler, the second some woman with a gynecological problem.

The man's name was Jairus. No doubt, he used his clout to get to Jesus. Shoving his way through the mass of humanity, he laid his request before the Master. "Please come quickly. My daughter is at death's door!" Jesus grants his request and the urgent march begins. You can hear Jairus and his servants say, "Clear the way. Move it! We've got an emergency. It's a matter of life and death . . . ."

Somewhere along the way, the train gets derailed by a frail woman. She didn't mean to stop the procession. All she wanted to do was siphon a little power off the fringe of Jesus' prayer shawl. Granted, it was a bit superstitious. But she believed that if she could grab the edge of his prayer tassel, some of his spiritual power would shoot into her body and heal her embarrassing bleeding. How a woman in her condition clawed through the crowd is mystifying . . . or maybe not. After all, this is not the sort of thing that can be kept hidden with third-world sanitary conditions. Most men would lunge out of the way. Nonetheless, she gets close enough to brush against the master — she and a hundred other folks!

Suddenly Jesus stops. You can imagine Jairus asked, "Whoa, what happened?" "Someone touched me," Jesus said. Peter piped up, "Uh, Lord . . . there are dozens of people touching you. Have you lost it?!" "No" Jesus answered, "Someone touched me with faith. I felt power go out from me." His eyes scan the crowd. The woman cowers. Jairus sighs. In the face of an urgent crisis, Jesus restores this woman back to society by publicly declaring her clean. It was a terribly kind thing to do, considering that such a bleeding condition would separate her from the synagogue, from her friends, even from her husband.

The problem is that it takes too long. By the time Jesus reverses this twelve-year-old condition, the twelve-year-old girl has died. The servants arrive and tell Jairus to release Jesus. His services are no longer needed nor sufficient (or so they think). Jesus lunges at Jairus, "Don't be afraid; just believe, and she will be healed." Sometimes we want to believe Jesus, but the voice of the crowd keeps echoing in our ears: "It's too late."

The parade proceeds to Jairus' house. Jesus interrupts a funeral already in progress. When he tells them *their* services are no longer needed, they actually laugh at him. No matter, he will get the last laugh. Inside the house, with Peter, James, and John (and the girl's parents, of course), Jesus orders her spirit to return to her body. The following celebration is predictable.

Little did they know, however, just how rich this encounter was. You see, Jesus' actions are larger than a couple of women and a trail of tears. These aren't merely miracles, they are prophecies. These two women mirror our own predicament. We will again see blood and death side by side at Golgotha. Jesus will take blood and death, that which most defiles, and undo their effects. These two females aren't the only beneficiaries of Jesus' power. This is the core of Jesus' ministry, to reverse the effects of blood and death through his very own.

Mark intends for us to see ourselves in the mirror of these women. Our rejoicing in Jesus should, therefore, be no less earnest than theirs.

Further Reading: Colossians 1:19-23.

Ponderable Questions: What were the social implications of blood and death in Jesus day? How do these two women represent your own life predicament, particularly before you came to Jesus? How much of the effects of "blood" and "death" has Jesus already removed from your life? What do you expect he will complete when he returns?

Considerations for Prayer: Find a hymnal. Look in the index for songs about blood. Allow them to guide your prayers to God.

Encounters with Christ

Breaking Away from Galilee

Feeding 5,000

{Mark 6:34,39-44; § 72}

When Jesus landed and saw a large crowd, he had compassion on them, because they were like sheep without a shepherd. So he began teaching them many things. . . Then Jesus directed them to have all the people sit down in groups on the green grass. So they sat down in groups of hundreds and fifties. Taking the five loaves and the two fish and looking up to heaven, he gave thanks and broke the loaves. Then he gave them to his disciples to set before the people. He also divided the two fish among them all. They all ate and were satisfied, and the disciples picked up twelve basketfuls of broken pieces of bread and fish. The number of the men who had eaten was five thousand.

Jesus' disciples had just come back from their itinerant preaching tour. It was a dandy! They had stories galore. Just imagine the one-upmanship between these fiercely competitive comrades. If Peter bragged about an exorcism, John would top it with a healing of a lame man. Matthew, of course, would have something to say about reaching more sinners than the rest. And Iscariot would add his two cents as well. Jesus likely just let them talk and enjoyed every minute of their success.

About that same time another group of disciples came to Jesus. These were John's hard-core followers who refused to abandon him. Even though John told them to follow Jesus, and even after he had been thrown into prison, they hang on for dear life until John's death. They come to Jesus with the gruesome news of John's beheading. He was more than a friend. John was the greatest man born of woman, the forerunner of the Messiah and the last Old Testament prophet. Jesus was visibly shaken.

Pressed between the joy of his own disciples and the demoralizing sadness of John's, Jesus decides that it's time for some R & R. They get into the boat and head across the lake. The clamoring crowds follow. You can hardly blame them, but their affection is oppressive. They notice the direction of the sails and set out on foot. Running a distance of ten miles, many were on crutches, others carried pallets. The fleet of foot arrive on the other side of the lake even before Jesus. Others are strewn along the shoreline for several miles, like ants heading to a picnic. There were thousands of them. Estimates generally run in the neighborhood of 15,000.

Jesus' overwhelming exhaustion was overcome by his compassion. Mark 6:34, one of the most endearing verses of the Scriptures says this: "When Jesus landed and saw a large crowd, he had compassion on them, because they were like sheep without a shepherd. So he began teaching them many things." His compassion didn't stop there; he also healed them. Then, as if this wasn't enough, he fed them. Not a bad example for ministry.

Strewn across the hills of budding green grass, the masses arranged themselves in groups of fifties and hundreds. It looked from heaven like a garden of humanity waiting to be cultivated by the Master. Jesus lifts the bread to heaven like the patriarch of a family and gives thanks to God for his provision. He begins to break the five small loaves for distribution. Before long the eyes of the disciples are wide with wonder. Their bewilderment spreads across the crowd like wildfire. You can almost hear the echoes of whispers erupt into praise. They were seeing with their own eyes the unveiling of God in their midst. The very Creator was at work. No wonder they wanted to make him king right then and there. No wonder all four Gospel writers record this event. It is simply massive. It is also deep. We're not merely looking at power, but also at promise.

This is Jesus' paradigmatic ministry — healing, teaching, feeding — loving the whole person. It is Jesus at his best when he is feeling his worst. It is a snapshot of his own sacrifice. "Where," you might ask, "is the timber? Where are the nails?" Oh, we're not on the hill yet; we're still in the upper room. This is Eucharistic. The bread is his body (John 6:54). He is not merely offering a free lunch. He is offering himself. Those who will ingest him will find that his life becomes their own. For all who have ever said, "Man, I wish I could have been there to watch him feed the masses," Jesus invites you to the table.

Further Reading: John 6:1-59.

Ponderable Questions: When was the last time you were too tired to really care about people? How is it that Jesus did not act the way we often do when we're tired? How does Jesus' feeding these people under these conditions give you hope for the present and promise for the future? How is this text echoed in the Eucharist?

Considerations for Prayer: Memorize Psalm 55:22 and/or I Peter 5:7. Talk to God about these texts.

Water-Walking Record Set

{Matthew 14:25-31; § 74}

During the fourth watch of the night Jesus went out to them, walking on the lake. When the disciples saw him walking on the lake, they were terrified. "It's a ghost," they said, and cried out in fear. But Jesus immediately said to them: "Take courage! It is I. Don't be afraid." "Lord, if it's you," Peter replied, "tell me to come to you on the water." "Come," he said. Then Peter got down out of the boat, walked on the water and came toward Jesus. But when he saw the wind, he was afraid and, beginning to sink, cried out, "Lord, save me!" Immediately Jesus reached out his hand and caught him. "You of little faith," he said, "why did you doubt?"

I have a confession to make. Shortly after I was baptized at 9 years old, I ran across this text and somehow combined it with the moving-mountains-by-prayer passage. I stood at the edge of our neighborhood swimming pool, closed my eyes and mustered my faith. After several moments I felt sufficiently "prayed up." I could almost hear the voice of my Lord beckoning me to come to him across the waves. Needless to say, my surfing stint was shorter than Simon's!

My interpretation of this passage was as lame as my water-walking record. But I did see two things correctly. First, I personalized Peter. As I looked into the passage I saw myself. This seems to be Matthew's intention, to hold up Peter as a mirror to our own experience. After all, much in this story is symbolic: a storm, fear, a call of Jesus, an outrageous step of faith. This is more than an historical incident, it is a microcosm of the Christian's quest. We want so badly to see Jesus, to walk with him through life's storm. Yet the waves distract us. We take our eyes off him and lose our footing.

This is, indeed, "our" story, not just Peter's. In fact, Matthew continues to trace Peter's faltering steps through the next five chapters. In

Matthew 15:15 he can't understand Jesus' parable. In 16:16-19 he makes a great confession but winds up badly misunderstanding Jesus' mission (vv. 22-23). Again, at the transfiguration, he foolishly wanted to build three tabernacles (17:4). And in 18:21 he thought he was generous with a sevenfold forgiveness only to find Jesus increasing it to 70×7. Peter's biography in these five chapters is checkered, to say the least. Perhaps that's why we like him so much. His biography is our autobiography.

There's a second thing I did right with this passage. Intuitively I knew that it was about faith. Unfortunately I took it to be faith in my own ability to accomplish phenomenal feats. This text is not about me. It is not even about Peter. It is about Jesus. This is seen back in verse 27. When the disciples shout, "It's a ghost!" Jesus replies, "It is I, don't be afraid." The second half of this phrase reminds us of what angels say when they appear. The first half reminds us of what God said to Moses (Exod. 3:14). When Moses needed a name to give to Pharaoh, God said, "Tell him my name is Yahweh — the ever-existing one." This was such a sacred name that the Jewish people wouldn't even say it out loud. Over time they even forgot how to pronounce it! This makes Jesus' statement all the more outrageous. Translated into Greek, this is a subtle, yet bold claim to deity.

Now, when one makes certain claims, he had better be able to back them up. Guess what. Jesus did just that. In fact, his actions speak louder than his words. The previous evening he acted like God the Creator, feeding 5,000 with a handful of dinner rolls. Here, sometime between 4 and 6 a.m., he acts like God the Sustainer, who hovers over the chaotic waters. Indeed, this Jesus is Yahweh. Because he is Yahweh, we can place our trust in him. His call to faith may be radical; it often is. Yet his call is never more radical nor more celestial than his own person.

Further Reading: Psalm 55:1-8; 107:29.

Ponderable Questions: Do you think it is fair to allegorize this text as the "storms of life" that Christians (like Peter) often face? Explain why and how far you might take it. Give an example from your own life that mirrors Peter's actions here. What do you do to "recover" once you've gotten back in the boat?

Considerations for Prayer: Confess to God the troubles you're experiencing. Plead with him, face to the ground if necessary, to sustain you and lift you from the waves. Sing "It Is Well with My Soul."

To Whom Shall We Go?

{John 6:26-29,52-54,66-69; § 76}

> Jesus answered, "I tell you the truth, you are looking for me, not because you saw miraculous signs but because you ate the loaves and had your fill. Do not work for food that spoils, but for food that endures to eternal life, which the Son of Man will give you. On him God the Father has placed his seal of approval." Then they asked him, "What must we do to do the works God requires?" Jesus answered, "The work of God is this: to believe in the one he has sent." . . . Then the Jews began to argue sharply among themselves, "How can this man give us his flesh to eat?" Jesus said to them, "I tell you the truth, unless you eat the flesh of the Son of Man and drink his blood, you have no life in you. Whoever eats my flesh and drinks my blood has eternal life, and I will raise him up at the last day . . . From this time many of his disciples turned back and no longer followed him. "You do not want to leave too, do you?" Jesus asked the Twelve. Simon Peter answered him, "Lord, to whom shall we go? You have the words of eternal life. We believe and know that you are the Holy One of God."

This has got to be the worst sermon Jesus ever preached. He starts out with literally thousands and winds up with merely a dozen. The problem, you see, is that Jesus expected too much from his audience. After feeding 5,000 the day before, such excitement is only natural. Jesus should have known they would be back for a repeat performance. Granted, he is tired, but still he seems a bit grumpy and his demands are bizarre. "Eat my flesh and drink my blood"?! Obviously this is a hyperbole. His listeners surely knew that. Even so, it's still kind of gross.

Why would Jesus say such things? Consider this: It is now two years into his ministry. This is one of those mile markers that separate casual fans from devoted followers. Verse 66 says "From this time many of his disciples turned back and no longer followed him." This is as it should be — as it needs to be. Jesus is apparently not nearly as interested in numbers as we. He rather prefers faith. In fact, he states,

"The work of God is this: to believe in the one he has sent" (v. 29). Don't underestimate how hard this work can be. To believe in Jesus, to truly trust him, leads one through some rather treacherous territory. It is a land filled with bizarre sayings and turbulent expectations. It will lead you through deep and stormy waters with but one thin sail in the shape of a cross. If your ship is not ready for such a journey, Jesus willingly drives her away.

With these radical words and extreme expectations, Jesus whittles the crowds down to a manageable handful. He then turns to the remnant and asks, "You do not want to leave too, do you?" (v. 67). It was almost as if Jesus was inviting them, or perhaps challenging them, to leave with the rest. Peter, as usual, is the first to speak. Often he trips over his tongue, but this time his words are brilliant. "Lord, to whom shall we go? You have the words of eternal life!" (v. 68).

Sometimes we follow Jesus because it all makes sense. There is often great reward in righteousness and great peace in grace. Let's be honest though. There are times when nothing makes sense, when Jesus' words are strange and dangerous. He seems out of touch or even out of sorts. There are seasons when we know next to nothing for certain. All seems cloudy and veiled. Yet this one thing we do know: Jesus has the words of life. His words don't always align with our reason. Yet they tower over our existence. He is the great I AM, the very bread from heaven (v. 35). No one else has done what he has done. No one else can speak the way he speaks. No one else can move us from earth to heaven in quite the way he can. His Spirit gives life, particularly when our flesh counts for nothing (v. 63). So we hold on by faith because, like it or not, he is the only option. To whom can we go? If Jesus is not who he claimed, we are, indeed, left lifeless.

Further Reading: 1 Corinthians 1:18-31.

Ponderable Questions: Have you ever found the words and demands of Jesus difficult, or even offensive? If you didn't follow Jesus, what would you do instead? What would you be? What is the next best thing to Jesus? List some of the words (statements/ideas) of Jesus that have given you life.

Considerations for Prayer: Confess to God any frustration you're having right now in following Jesus. Confess to him you have no other good options but to be faithful to him.

Garbage In, Garbage Out

{Mark 7:1-2,5-8,15; § 77}

The Pharisees and some of the teachers of the law who had come from Jerusalem gathered around Jesus and saw some of his disciples eating food with hands that were "unclean," that is, unwashed. . . . So the Pharisees and teachers of the law asked Jesus, "Why don't your disciples live according to the tradition of the elders instead of eating their food with 'unclean' hands?" He replied, "Isaiah was right when he prophesied about you hypocrites; as it is written: 'These people honor me with their lips,/ but their hearts are far from me./ They worship me in vain;/ their teachings are but rules taught by men.' You have let go of the commands of God and are holding on to the traditions of men . . . . Nothing outside a man can make him 'unclean' by going into him. Rather, it is what comes out of a man that makes him 'unclean.'"

Why on earth would the biblical authors choose to tell us about Jesus' table manners? So he didn't wash before he ate, big deal! Apparently it was. The religious teachers at the time were meticulous about ritual washing before meals. Understand that this was not for good hygiene. Germs hadn't even been invented yet. No, this had nothing to do with science. It was all about religion. You see, they believed that some kind of spiritual defilement could be purified with ritual water. So they drew up specific rules as to how one should go about this ceremonial washing. In essence, they were not purging germs, they were building fences. These religious fences defined who was in and who was out. Jesus is assailing the whole fence, not just breaking a board of it.

Morality for the Jews was all about the fence. It made a box. At the center of the box was pure and undefiled religion. It was a kind of contest to see who could get closest to the center of the box. The more rules you kept, the closer to dead center you were. Jesus came along and proposed a new mode of morality. Instead of fences, he suggested compassion. Here's the problem: the fences effectively kept people out. Compassion, however, required that the fences be dismantled. The truly religious person then left the compound and purposely sought out the very scalawags the fences once kept out. Thus, Jesus is not tweaking their ethical system, he is demolishing it!

Formerly, one was religious by abstaining from food. Now one is religious by what comes from the heart. Before, religion was external. Now it is internal. Within the fence, one is constrained by rules. Outside the fence, one is compelled by love. The difference is colossal. This new mode of ethics is both liberating and frightening. And frankly, it is dangerous. It is dangerous because it has fewer controls. Who can know what sort of people might be welcomed into the fellowship? Who can control their illicit behaviors without clear rules? Why, they might smoke in the bathroom at church or pierce body parts that only show up in the baptistery. Furthermore, you never know where compassion might take you. Simply put, compassion is not prudent.

Our own list of rules, strikingly similar to that of the Jews, is a good list. After all, smoking is bad for you. Body piercing is a bit macabre. Drinking is dangerous, and church attendance is good. So what's so bad about a few good rules?! Why is Jesus so violently opposed to morality by lists? Because bad men keep good rules and it makes them feel good about their evil hearts. We freely commit these sins Jesus lists because we artificially keep a moral list of our own making. Thus bad men appear good because their external morality shrouds their internal iniquity.

There's something more. When Jesus declares all foods clean, the topic turns out to be ethnic groups not food groups. By the time Acts rolls around, this passage surfaces again. It is interpreted apostolically (cf. Acts 10:9-15). Guess what: The context is not about table manners, but table fellowship. Had it merely been food, it wouldn't be worth the bother. Since it is about people, it is embedded in Scripture. Listen to Jesus' conclusion: "From within, out of men's hearts, come evil thoughts, sexual immorality, theft, murder, adultery, greed, malice, deceit, lewdness, envy, slander, arrogance and folly. All these evils come from inside and make a man 'unclean.'" The bottom line is this: Our moral lists wind up separating us from the very people who need compassion. Then, as if that weren't bad enough, we justify sinning against these very people in the ways Jesus just mentioned. Why are we so blind to our own attitudes and sins? Because it's hard to see much from inside a box.

Further Reading: Mark 7:1-23; Isaiah 29:1-19.

Ponderable Questions: Can you think of a time that your

behavior was "kosher" but your heart was not right? Describe the moral boxes of your church that artificially define what is good and what is bad. How do these boxes keep outsiders away from God? How do they fool us into thinking we are good when, in fact, we are being offensive to God?

Considerations for Prayer: Ask God to grant you prophetic insight into his priorities for his people without being obnoxious, cynical or critical of the church which is his bride.

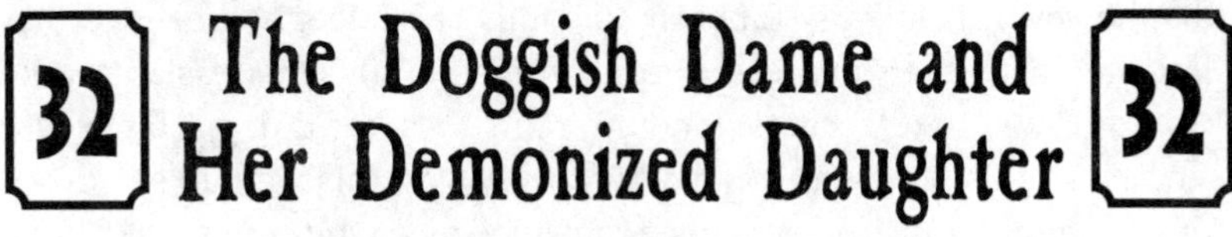

{Matthew 15:22-28; § 78}

> A Canaanite woman from that vicinity came to him, crying out, "Lord, Son of David, have mercy on me! My daughter is suffering terribly from demon-possession." Jesus did not answer a word. So his disciples came to him and urged him, "Send her away, for she keeps crying out after us." He answered, "I was sent only to the lost sheep of Israel." The woman came and knelt before him. "Lord, help me!" she said. He replied, "It is not right to take the children's bread and toss it to their dogs." "Yes, Lord," she said, "but even the dogs eat the crumbs that fall from their masters' table." Then Jesus answered, "Woman, you have great faith! Your request is granted." And her daughter was healed from that very hour.

He called the woman a DOG! That's the sort of thing one expects from a redneck, not the master of liberation. It's even more degrading considering the Jewish view of dogs. They were unclean scavengers! Why is Jesus so rough with the old gal?

Take a look at her portrait. She is from the area of Tyre and Sidon. These cities were the epitome of Israel's ancient enemies. She is a Canaanite. Her ancestors were a scourge on the land. Because of their immorality God drove them out. She is a woman in an androcentric society. Worse yet, her daughter has a demon. She isn't just wearing a black hat in this portrait, it is pointy and she sits on a broom! She could hardly be pictured in a worse light.

She ferrets out Jesus in this Jewish home. What's he doing there? Hiding, apparently. The Pharisees have followed Jesus throughout Galilee. Their pestering political pressure is white hot. The Lord goes underground with his disciples. Things need to cool off. But they don't. Rumors of this evangelist-healer permeate the region. Crowds of invalids converge upon Jesus' hideout. This woman sneaks in among some of the sick. She doesn't really belong, but where else is she to go? As one might suspect, she is rather persistent. The disciples have had enough. They usher her in to Jesus and beg him to get rid of her before she wears them out.

Jesus stoutly refuses. He has nothing to do with her. He was in the throes of his ministry to the Jews. There is no time for distractions. She, however, is just as stubborn. She falls at his feet and begs for her daughter. She even addresses Jesus with the kosher Messianic title, "Son of David." He accepts none of it and calls her a dog. This would send most gals scurrying off in a huff. However, this woman's concern for her daughter overpowers her ego. Quick as a whip she says, "I may be a dog, but even they eat scraps from the master's table." That was a perfect reply. While Jews did not have dogs as pets, Gentiles did. She admits, "I don't belong in the family, but surely there is room for a little leftover compassion."

Jesus is not impressed by much. In fact, faith is about the only thing that moves *this* mountain! Here's a woman full of faith. Jesus is moved. Her daughter is healed.

So why does Jesus call her a dog? Isn't that kind of rude? Perhaps, but look where it led. The woman came in search of a healing, she left with a Lord. He doesn't want to be a mere miracle worker. He demands to be Messiah. By calling her names he clarifies who she is in relation to him. He will not allow his ministry to be reduced to a sideshow. Once she understood his role, Jesus moved swiftly and decisively on her behalf.

I suppose her story is not far removed from our own. When we come with our own agendas and petty requests, we're not much better than petulant canines. Only when Jesus is truly Lord are we welcomed as citizens to the table of the kingdom.

Further Reading: Isaiah 2:2; 42:6; 49:6; "Passages of Gentile Inclusion" — available in electronic form from College Press.

Ponderable Questions: Why did Jesus not grant this woman's request immediately? What kind of agendas do we often approach Jesus with? Realistically, what would happen to our faith, both good and bad, if Jesus gave us all we asked for? How would this alter our perception of who Jesus is?

Considerations for Prayer: Don't ask for anything. Just tell Jesus who you understand him to be.

Leaven, Loaves, and Leaders

{Matthew 16:5-12; § 81a}

When they went across the lake, the disciples forgot to take bread. "Be careful," Jesus said to them. "Be on your guard against the yeast of the Pharisees and Sadducees." They discussed this among themselves and said, "It is because we didn't bring any bread." Aware of their discussion, Jesus asked, "You of little faith, why are you talking among yourselves about having no bread? Do you still not understand? Don't you remember the five loaves for the five thousand, and how many basketfuls you gathered? . . . Then they understood that he was not telling them to guard against the yeast used in bread, but against the teaching of the Pharisees and Sadducees.

On the southwest shore of Galilee Jesus pulls up to a little place called Magadan. His recent flurry of miracles has created quite a stir. The Pharisees who came from Jerusalem finally catch up to him. He had been avoiding them by going underground in Gentile territory. When he emerges here in Magadan, the Pharisees have found reinforcements. They are aligned with the Sadducees as well as the Herodians (Mark 8:15). Bottom line: Jesus has aggravated just about every religious and political party out there.

They come with a request . . . okay, maybe it was a demand. "You need to back up your claims with a sign!" This was nothing new. Four other times in the Gospels Jewish leaders say the same thing to Jesus (John 2:18-23; 6:30; Matt. 12:38-45; and Luke 11:16,29). This seems to be a fairly common occurrence in Jesus' ministry.

It may seem odd that they would ask for a sign. After all, didn't Jesus do signs all the time? Yes, but in their way of thinking, every new claim had to be backed up individually. It is kind of like credit cards. Just because one is authorized at the checkout counter, does not mean they will accept a second without checking it out, too. As Jesus becomes more clear in his Messianic claims, the leaders more earnestly seek verification.

Jesus, however, knows their hearts. They want excuses, not evidence. He won't pander to disbelief. All he offers is the sign of Jonah. Granted, this refers to the resurrection which is phenomenal verification. But the sign of Jonah to the Ninevites was also a message of damnation. Without faith, even these leaders are lost. They are probably pretty unhappy about being compared to the Ninevites. Jesus doesn't seem too concerned. He turns and walks away.

He and the band get in a boat and off they go. Jesus is still a bit miffed by the encounter and says, "Guard against the leaven of the Pharisees!" He is speaking metaphorically, of course. He's not talking about their bread, but their doctrine. Jesus' warning spans the political gamut from Pharisees to Sadducees to Herodians. On the surface, each of these three religiopolitical parties teaches radically different things. Yet they are all cut from the same cloth in this: They demand a sign from Jesus. They *act* as if they would follow him. Yet their feigned allegiance is a farce. Jesus warns, "You watch out for that."

The disciples aren't watching much of anything right now. The mere mention of bread reminds them of how hungry they are. Somebody dropped the ball. There's nothing to eat in the boat save one measly loaf. That won't do!

Jesus interrupts, "Your faith is SO small." He had just fed the 4,000 as an encore to the 5,000, and these guys fret because they only have one loaf! In Jesus' hands that's enough to sink the ship! Here's what's so sad about the loaves and why it's combined with the sign-seeking Sadducees. The disciples of Jesus, his closest friends, have no clearer idea of his identity than do his enemies. Both the Apostles and the Pharisees lacked faith. Do we really fare better? We act like we understand who he is. We arrogate ourselves over his enemies. But how do we really stack up? How often we ask for signs. How frequently we need verification, clarification, or an occupational itinerary. We stew over food in the presence of the Bread of Life. One ought not to worry about the mundane in the presence of the Eternal.

Further Reading: Psalm 78; "Jewish Sects" — available in electronic form from College Press.

Ponderable Questions: What "signs" has Jesus given us of his existence and power that we tend to ignore? Can you remember a time you asked God to "prove" himself to you? What was the result? What "bread" in your life is in danger of distracting you from the presence of the Eternal One?

Considerations for Prayer: Recount to God all the wonderful things he has done for you.

The Rock of Ages

{Matthew 16:13-18; § 82}

When Jesus came to the region of Caesarea Philippi, he asked his disciples, "Who do people say the Son of Man is?" They replied, "Some say John the Baptist; others say Elijah; and still others, Jeremiah or one of the prophets." "But what about you?" he asked. "Who do you say I am?" Simon Peter answered, "You are the Christ, the Son of the living God." Jesus replied, "Blessed are you, Simon son of Jonah, for this was not revealed to you by man, but by my Father in heaven. And I tell you that you are Peter, and on this rock I will build my church, and the gates of Hades will not overcome it.

Sometimes our confession becomes our commission. This usually happens during defining moments of our lives. For example, when a young groom says "I do," there is more at play than a confession of love. This is his commission to matrimony. In a sense, Peter stands here at the altar with Jesus. They have been together for 2+ years now. It is time for a defining moment. It is time for a clear confession, which will become Peter's commission.

Jesus & Co. head north. This is the farthest he has ever traveled outside Jewish territory. That's a bit nerve-racking to the troops since it comes at the low ebb of Jesus' popularity. You can just imagine the questions that race through their minds. "Is he bugging out? Is he going to quit? What is he thinking?"

Jesus turns and asks this question: "Who do people say that I am?" Two things should be apparent. First, Jesus doesn't need to be omniscient to figure this out. Rumors about him fly at high decibels. Second, it really doesn't matter what others say about him. He tends not to change with the winds of popularity. Clearly Jesus is not asking this question because the disciples can somehow help him figure it out. His question is for their benefit, not his.

The first question pulls them together, the second penetrates their soul. "Who do YOU say that I am?" This is the only question that really mattered and one we will all have to answer. Peter responds as a representative for the group. "You are the Christ, the Son of the Living God." Now Simon had frequently fumbled with his words. This time, however, his tongue is golden. In fact, Jesus recognizes that such a great confession comes only from the Father.

As beautiful as it is, confession is not enough. It must move to commission. So Jesus presses Peter at three points. First, he is to become the foundation of the church. Obviously he doesn't stand alone; the other Apostles will be by his side (Eph. 2:20). Yet just as he represents them in his confession, so too he represents the group as the foundation of the church. Second, he has the keys. Again, Peter is not alone responsible for apostolic preaching, but he does take the lead on the day of Pentecost (Acts 2) and at Cornelius's house (Acts 10). Third, through his preaching, he will declare forgiveness of sins. Here on earth he will enact the decrees of heaven. Such is Peter's role.

Here's the catch: At this point Peter doesn't merely represent the Twelve. He represents every follower of Jesus. His confession becomes ours. He blazed the trail through which we all travel. Every follower must pass this same gate that declares Jesus as the Christ, the Son of the living God. Moreover, if Peter's confession becomes our own, so does his commission. He laid the foundation, we build on top of it. He unlocked the door, we lead people through it. He proclaimed God's forgiveness of sins on earth, we reiterate it. The confession of Christ has not changed, nor has his commission. We too are divine ambassadors, announcing God's forgiveness through the blood of Jesus (2 Cor. 5:20). If we believe what we say about Jesus, how could we not then announce his redemption to the waiting world?

Further Reading: 1 Timothy 3:16.

Ponderable Questions: What are some of the things people these days say about who Jesus is? What do you believe about Jesus? List those people you come into contact with in an average week. How many of them have heard your confession of Christ?

Considerations for Prayer: Ask God to reveal his Son to you as he did to Peter.

The Prediction of Passion

{Matthew 16:21-25; § 83}

From that time on Jesus began to explain to his disciples that he must go to Jerusalem and suffer many things at the hands of the elders, chief priests and teachers of the law, and that he must be killed and on the third day be raised to life. Peter took him aside and began to rebuke him. "Never, Lord!" he said. "This shall never happen to you!" Jesus turned and said to Peter, "Get behind me, Satan! You are a stumbling block to me; you do not have in mind the things of God, but the things of men." Then Jesus said to his disciples, "If anyone would come after me, he must deny himself and take up his cross and follow me. For whoever wants to save his life will lose it, but whoever loses his life for me will find it.

Peter has just made the "great confession." It was a great day! Jesus had longed for this for a very long time. Finally, after 2+ years, the disciples openly articulate their faith in Jesus. They got it . . . finally! As wonderful as this is, however, it presents a grave danger. Their image of the Messiah was skewed. They thought he would conquer through power. Jesus, however, envisions victory through the cross. He hastens to clarify his agenda before these boys run too far down the path of zeal instead of passion. They are much more drawn to the sword than the cross.

This idea of a suffering Messiah was a blistering bombshell for the disciples. Intent on conquest, they never envisioned suffering. How could the Messiah be successful if he were betrayed? How could he rule if he were assassinated? How could he marshal an army if he couldn't defend himself? The answer is simple but paradoxical: the Christ conquers through a cross. Jesus' humiliating defeat is our proclamation of victory.

The cross has been clouded by centuries of distortion. It has become a trinket. It is plated with gold and draped delicately across the chests of beautiful women. It is polished and veneered to adorn our churches. It has been emblazoned on shields of soldiers and plastered on the bumpers of our cars. Today it represents beauty, power, and success. In Jesus' day it represented suffering, ugliness, and defeat. Oh, cross of Christ, you've come a long way, baby!

If perchance the church seems to be missing something, perhaps it is the cross. The decorated shell is still there, but the core of the cross has been sucked dry. We somehow imagine that we will find success through power and manipulation, through skill and beauty. Jesus disagrees. His example to us is also his call: "Take up your cross and follow me. If anyone wants to save his life, he will lose it; and if anyone loses his life for my sake, he will find it." This is a paradoxical economy. Yet this is the upside-down world in which the Christian thrives. We live through death. We are first by being last. We are greatest when we serve. Above all, we conquer through the cross. Through self-abnegation and purposeful surrender we rise above all that would seduce us to the mundane. If you wonder why your life lacks power, perhaps it is because you've not yet died. If you long for victory, lay down your aspirations. If you seek significance, become nothing. All our attempts at self-aggrandizement are blatant accusations that Jesus is a liar. His path is the Way of the Cross. He walked no other way. He left no other trail save this one, stained by blood. Follow it, for it is the only path to life.

Further Reading: Matthew 5:3-12; "Passion Predictions"—available in electronic form from College Press.

Ponderable Questions: Explain this statement: "The cross is not an historic event but a way of life." What are some of the misconceptions in the church about the cross? Is it really true that the way to victory is through suffering? What might that mean to American Christians?

Considerations for Prayer: Walk through the beatitudes and ask God for guidance in how to incorporate them into your existence.

36 A Momentous Mountain 36

{Luke 9:28-31,35; § 85}

About eight days after Jesus said this, he took Peter, John and James with him and went up onto a mountain to pray. As he was praying, the appearance of his face changed, and his clothes became as bright as a flash of lightning. Two men, Moses and Elijah, appeared in glorious splendor, talking with Jesus. They spoke about his departure, which he was about to bring to fulfillment at Jerusalem. . . . A voice came from the cloud, saying, "This is my Son, whom I have chosen; listen to him."

There is no other event in the life of Jesus that is so well-connected to the whole. The transfiguration, in a sense, is the biography of Jesus in a nutshell. Here we hear echoes of baptism through the heavenly voice. The prophets stand as reminders of the predictions of the coming Messiah. The three alone with Jesus on a mountain foreshadow Gethsemane. The conversation between Jesus and the heavenly visitors centered around his death in Jerusalem. His transformed countenance sheds light on the resurrection. And the cloud on the mountain reminds us of his ascension. These connections are uncanny. This is the closest to heaven that Jesus ever got on earth. From this summit we can survey his entire life and ministry.

Matthew and Mark both suggest that it is a colossal event by placing it on the seventh day (Matt. 17:1; Mark 9:2). In Jewish vernacular, that's when the "big stuff" happened. Other textual clues point in the same direction: The voice of God, the high mountain, the appearance of Moses and Elijah, and the dazzling bright light. In many ways this was the pinnacle of Jesus' ministry. It apparently made quite an impression on Peter. He wanted to preserve the moment by erecting a lean-to for each of his three heroes. He is, of course, rebuked for his foolishness. (Although we might want to cut him some slack. He was too scared at the time to really think straight [Mark 9:6]). This has obviously been a bad week for Peter. First Jesus calls him Satan. Now God himself chides him.

So what's the point? Granted, it is an engaging tale. With all the bright lights and spooky ghosts, it's an attention grabber. Yet surely it is deeper than some strange bedtime story. There is a pattern developing here. (A) Peter confesses Jesus as God's Son. (B) Jesus reveals his impending death in Jerusalem. (A) Jesus is transfigured on a mountain. (B) Coming down the mountain he predicts he will suffer just like "Elijah" (a.k.a. "John the Baptist"). Jesus' identity is finally unfolding before the disciples. As it does, two things must happen. First, Jesus must connect his suffering with his glory — the cross must be woven into the crown. Second, because this was paradoxical and perplexing to the Apostles, they would need special verification to substantiate this suffering Messiah.

Jesus *is* the Messiah. Jesus *will* suffer. These seemingly contradictory statements must be proven. God knew that, and he provided nothing short of a transfiguration. His own voice thundered the declaration: Listen to HIM. As great as Moses was, this suffering Messiah is greater still. As wonderful as Elijah was, this one destined to die was yet more marvelous.

This is just the validation the Apostles needed. We need it too. Oh, not every day. Most of the time, in fact, we are pretty confident that Jesus is Lord. We get along just fine, trusting that he is in control. But, when our lives get out of control, we question whether he is still in control. These are the times when our faith is shaken. When life doesn't pan out like planned, questions begin to leach to the surface. Oddly enough, it is when we suffer — like Jesus — that we are most vulnerable to doubt. "This shouldn't happen to me," we protest, not knowing that this is precisely the path that Jesus walked. How strange that when our lives most mirror Christ's, we question the validity of his identity. It is in these valleys that we most need to remember the mountain.

Further Reading: Matthew 17:1-8; 2 Peter 1:16-18.

Ponderable Questions: When was the last time you were in a valley of despair? How did God reveal himself to you? What do you think Jesus talked with Elijah and Moses about? How should their conversations guide our own when we are going through periods of doubt and/or despair?

Considerations for Prayer: Sing "Open My Eyes, Lord."

From Failure to Faith 37

{Mark 9:17-19,22b-24; § 87}

"Teacher, I brought you my son, who is possessed by a spirit that has robbed him of speech. Whenever it seizes him, it throws him to the ground. He foams at the mouth, gnashes his teeth and becomes rigid. I asked your disciples to drive out the spirit, but they could not." "O unbelieving generation," Jesus replied, "how long shall I stay with you? How long shall I put up with you? Bring the boy to me." . . . "But if you can do anything, take pity on us and help us." "'If you can?'" said Jesus. "Everything is possible for him who believes." Immediately the boy's father exclaimed, "I do believe; help me overcome my unbelief!"

Coming home from church camp was always such a letdown. At camp there were singing, campfires, and Bible study, without any radios, TVs or computer games. One tends to make promises at camp that are difficult to keep. "God, I'll never shout at my brother again." Or "Lord, I'll read my Bible every day." Generally it doesn't take too long after the church van pulls into the parking lot for reality to set in. Your parents are still overbearing, and your brother is still a geek. Little temptations soon loom large.

This must be how Jesus and his trio feel coming down this mountain. They have had a once-in-a-lifetime, extraordinary experience. As they descend the steeps, they hear the din of an angry argument. The Pharisees are sneering and jeering. The disciples are whining and pining. The demonized boy is rolling in the dust and bellowing inarticulate guttural sounds. Jesus shakes his head in disbelief. All interested parties accost Jesus. The disciples want help; the Pharisees want to gloat; the crowds just want another miracle matinee.

The poor father is the only one who really seems to understand the gravity of the situation. He pleads with Jesus, "If you can do anything, take pity on us and help." Now, you might assume that the king of compassion would break down in tears, embrace the father, and heal his son. He doesn't. Instead he just goes off: "If you can?!" This is one of those incidents where vocal inflection is pretty important. If we could only have been there. Did Jesus say, "If you CAN?!, What do you mean? Do you doubt my ability?" Or did he say, "If YOU can. I'm able to do it . . . Are you able to receive it?" Either way, the issue is not really demon possession. Nor is it Jesus' miraculous ministry. The point is about faith.

The father's reply is the heart cry of most would-be followers of Jesus. "I do believe; help me overcome my unbelief." We want so badly to trust Jesus. We want so much to receive the fullness of his blessings. We just seem so inept, so unable to accept his truth. Jesus receives this mustard seed faith and grows it into a healing for his son. The father is overjoyed; the crowd is amazed.

Back inside the house the disciples corner Jesus. "What went wrong?" they asked. "Why couldn't we cast this demon out?" Perhaps they were looking for some secret incantation, some powerful exorcistic ceremony. Jesus gives them nothing but prayer. "Armed with this alone," Jesus says, "you could even move this mountain." (Scenes of the transfiguration must have flashed through three minds).

This story has several tributaries. It runs through prayer and exorcisms, past the Pharisees and the disciples. But ultimately it is all about faith. The disciples and the father have the very same problem. They lack faith. Whether we are the helpless victim or the powerless preacher, the problem is singular — we simply don't trust God enough. His power is sufficient. It's our faith that flounders. Belief births prayer, prayer encounters God, God moves mountains. For something so simple, this seems to be our most difficult task as Christians, simply to believe God.

Further Reading: 2 Kings 4:1-7; Galatians 3:6-14.

Ponderable Questions: Think about a time when you had real faith in God and did what he asked you to do. What were the results? Why do we have such a difficult time believing God? Why is it impossible to please God without faith (Heb. 11:4)?

Considerations for Prayer: Request that God would place an opportunity in your life this next week to live out real, dynamic faith in him. Be careful — he will answer this prayer.

38 Who Will Be Greatest? 38

{Mark 9:35-37; § 90}

"If anyone wants to be first, he must be the very last, and the servant of all." He took a little child and had him stand among them. Taking him in his arms, he said to them, "Whoever welcomes one of these little children in my name welcomes me; and whoever welcomes me does not welcome me but the one who sent me."

Part of me is a little disappointed in the Apostles. Another part of me empathizes more than I would like to admit. Here is the first of three times they argue about their relative greatness. It is more offensive, I suppose, since we have been indoctrinated to honor humility. We have been so "Christianized" that we balk at any display of pride. After all, the greatest is the least, the first is the last, and the humble exalted. Jesus embodied humility, and God demands it. Even the most secular of our nation can't even receive a trophy or an award without feeling obligated to thank God first.

Humility is a deeply entrenched cultural value. Deeper still is our rampant arrogance. This creates a paradox. Outwardly, we are trained to feign humility. Behind the scenes, however, we are groomed to promote ourselves. Coaches at little league and gymnastics, soccer moms and school sponsors goad us to seek self and win big. Products are sold by soliciting our egos — "Look out for #1," "If it feels good, do it," "It's expensive, but you're worth it." Athletes, politicians, and preachers provide adequate models for how to place oneself center stage. In the limelight of this ostensibly humble, but egregiously self-centered society, Jesus' words are merely a faint echo against the clamorous din of self-promotion. Nevertheless, his radical call to the abolition of self is essential to discipleship. One cannot be his disciple without this pivotal act of taking up a cross.

This argument is all the more offensive coming on the heels of Jesus' second passion prediction. The fact is, all three times this discussion arises, it follows Jesus' prediction of the cross. How strange! The Master keeps reminding them of his impending sacrifice, and they keep asking which is the greatest. This would be laughable if it weren't so contemporary.

Well, they asked a question, so Jesus gives them an answer. He picks up a child and sets him on his lap. This little guy had no legal status. Such was the lot of Palestinian children. They were to be seen and not heard. They were loved, but they were also considered property of the household, not quite persons. In fact, the Greek word for "child" doubled also as the word for "slave." "This one," Jesus said, "is the greatest among you." This helpless, powerless, fragile person was the epitome of a kingdom potentate. This is an upside-down kingdom for sure.

The question that follows is obvious. "What makes a child so great?" Jesus never answers it in the text. But the tenor of his ministry surely points in these directions. First and foremost, children have an uncompromising trust in their fathers. Because of their helpless estate, they are forced to cast themselves on the mercy of their father for sustenance and protection. Not a bad image for the believer. Second, they are incapable of jockeying for position and status. They know they are weak. Thus, they hide behind a very strong father. Were Christians to do the same, they would be impenetrable. Third, children are colorblind, impervious to dirt, ignorant of age, and unimpressed by credentials. They look in people's eyes in order to judge their souls. Is it any wonder that Jesus calls us back to pristine childhood as a prerequisite for entering the kingdom?

Further Reading: Matthew 6:1-18; "Childlike" — available in electronic form from College Press.

Ponderable Questions: What kinds of things do we do to gain status from other Christians or to raise ourselves to prominence in the church? What are some of the potential consequences if we are successful in doing so? Is self-seeking really that bad? State, in your own words, the "theology of humility."

Considerations for Prayer: Sing: "Make Me Like You, Lord."

39 Discouraging Disciples 39

{Matthew 8:19-22; § 93}

Then a teacher of the law came to him and said, "Teacher, I will follow you wherever you go." Jesus replied, "Foxes have holes and birds of the air have nests, but the Son of Man has no place to lay his head." Another disciple said to him, "Lord, first let me go and bury my father." But Jesus told him, "Follow me, and let the dead bury their own dead."

This incident is full of surprises. It is surprising that anyone would want to follow Jesus at this time. He has just come from the Feast of Tabernacles in Jerusalem (John 7–9) where he created quite a stir. Oh sure, plenty of people loved him. But there is a serious difference between loving Jesus and following him. It is one thing to admire the man. It is an entirely different thing to sacrifice for him. And speaking of sacrifice, we can't be much more than five months away from the cross. In fact, the Jewish leaders tried nearly a half a dozen times to arrest and/or kill Jesus in the past week alone. That's why it's such a shock that anyone would want to follow him. Besides, Judea is pretty dusty, and Jesus is planning a loosely scheduled preaching tour of her villages. That's no dream vacation.

More surprising still is that a Pharisee (i.e., "a teacher of the law") wanted to follow Jesus. Apparently they weren't all antagonistic to Jesus. In spite of the obvious ridicule and abuse that he would have to endure, this Pharisee wants to throw in with the Galilean band of Nazarenes. His request is appropriately dignified for one of his stature: I will follow you wherever you go. WOW! What more could Jesus ask? Plenty, apparently. This Pharisee was used to a good deal of creature comforts . . . like a bed and a house. Jesus doesn't have that to offer. In a surprising twist, Jesus rejected one of the only men actually qualified to serve him. (The only real "quality" person he has left now is Judas.)

A second man comes to Jesus with a request. Apparently, he has already been following Jesus for a while. At least he is called a "disciple." He wants to go bury his father. Since Palestinians buried their dead within hours of their death, it is unlikely that this man's father just died. Surely he would have been at the funeral already. We're not exactly sure what is going on here, but there are two pretty good possibilities. Perhaps his father is on his deathbed waiting to die. Or perhaps this disciple wants to wait around for the end of the typical year of Jewish mourning. Either way, by the time this fellow has finished his personal business, Jesus will have his own burial. This disciple can either follow now or never. With 20/20 hindsight, Jesus' words make a lot of sense. In the moment, however, they bordered on vicious. Obligations to family were sacred, even God-ordained. Jesus is making the bodacious claim to be more sacred than God's institution of family. Many in his audience would be repulsed. (Of course this is nothing new for Jesus).

Two men want to follow Jesus. The first is an outsider wanting in. The second is an insider temporarily wanting out. Both are rejected because they were distracted. It wasn't that they didn't love Jesus — clearly they did. It wasn't that they refused to sacrifice for Jesus — clearly they would. It was simply that something stood between them and Jesus. Here's the axiom that rises from this text: Jesus doesn't just want to be number one in your life; he wants to be the ONLY one in your life. Anything less is unacceptable; every distraction is detrimental.

Further Reading: Luke 9:57-62.

Ponderable Questions: Can you think of other incidents in the Gospels where Jesus made radical, almost unreasonable demands? In light of these men's rejection, do you think you would have measured up and been allowed to follow Jesus during his ministry? What would have to change before he would let you pursue him? Is your personal discipleship too comfortable?

Considerations for Prayer: "Holy Spirit, point out to me one thing in my life that is hindering me from full following. Then help me get rid of it. Be gentle . . . or maybe not."

40 Sibling Rivalry 40

{John 7:2-5; § 94-95}

When the Jewish Feast of Tabernacles was near, Jesus' brothers said to him, "You ought to leave here and go to Judea, so that your disciples may see the miracles you do. No one who wants to become a public figure acts in secret. Since you are doing these things, show yourself to the world." For even his own brothers did not believe in him.

For the past six months Jesus has been in hiding. He moved quickly from place to place, camping mostly in Gentile territory. Why? He was purposely avoiding a nasty confrontation with the Jewish leaders. Besides that, this relative anonymity also gave him time to invest in his chosen few. It was an important period of his ministry, but it is now time to come out in the open. As a result, six months from now he will be dead.

Jesus' half-brothers are frustrated, perhaps even livid. As the oldest son, Jesus is supposed to be responsible for the family's welfare. Instead, he has abandoned them. There are bills to pay, and his little escapade as some Messianic pretender is not helping. Furthermore, he is an embarrassment to the family. All these claims about being God's Son are attracting the wrong kind of attention. To make matters worse, when they went to confront him about it, he wouldn't even talk to them (Matt. 12:46-50). He simply must be stopped. This little charade has gone on long enough.

James, Joseph, Judas, and Simon catch up with Jesus on one of his brief appearances in Galilee. They challenge him to go up with them to the Feast of Tabernacles. He really ought to. After all, he missed the last Passover in Jerusalem. It has been eighteen months since he showed up in the capital city. Good Jews don't miss that many feasts, you know. If he is going to call himself Messiah, he must make his claim at Jerusalem. It is there he must be inaugurated.

Jesus has little interest in their expectations. He is too fiercely loyal to God's. As worldly men, Jesus' siblings can come and go as they please. Jesus, however, is constrained by a divine timetable; he has a higher agenda that controls his calendar. Eventually he will go up to this feast, but only when prompted by the Spirit of God, not when goaded by jealous rivals.

This lesson has not been learned well by Jesus' contemporary brothers. Because of our kinship (albeit by adoption), we often feel free to tell Jesus where to go and what to do. He is seldom more responsive to our importunity than he was to his siblings'. We should know better. Jesus is bound by his father's agenda, yet we pretend that he is at our beck and call. Like James, Joseph, Judas, and Simon, we have a well-defined image of who Jesus is supposed to be and how he is supposed to act. When he lets us down, we get indignant. We begin to give him "what for" and clearly outline our demands. When he shrugs us off, we retire in a huff, mumbling something under our breath about how mistreated we are. One must be cautious here. Jesus *will* show up at the feast. Our petty demands will dissipate while his will loom large and for a very long time. The lesson is simple: God sets the agenda for Jesus, and he for us. Ours is to follow; his, to direct.

Further Reading: John 7:1-13.

Ponderable Questions: In what ways has the church tried to manhandle Jesus? That is, how have we tried to direct him rather than being directed by him? Why did his brother's think they had claim to his life? How are we similar to them?

Considerations for Prayer: Walk through a list of things you control and submit each one to God.

Encounters with Christ

The Later Judean Ministry

Outrageous Claims of Christ – Part 1

{John 7:14-15,37-39; § 96}

Not until halfway through the Feast did Jesus go up to the temple courts and begin to teach. The Jews were amazed and asked, "How did this man get such learning without having studied?" . . . On the last and greatest day of the Feast, Jesus stood and said in a loud voice, "If anyone is thirsty, let him come to me and drink. Whoever believes in me, as the Scripture has said, streams of living water will flow from within him." By this he meant the Spirit, whom those who believed in him were later to receive. Up to that time the Spirit had not been given, since Jesus had not yet been glorified.

It was one of the most heated arguments that Jesus ever had. It lasted for more than a year and a half. That's probably long enough to move from an argument into a feud. It all started the last time he was in Jerusalem and healed some lame guy on the Sabbath. That, of course, ruffled a few feathers because Jesus disregarded ritual in preference for compassion. However, like most prolonged altercations, this one has evolved well beyond the original argument. Most of Jesus' enemies have long since forgotten when and why this started. All they know now is that Jesus is making claims that border on blasphemy, and many people believe him. This just won't do. Theology aside, he is infringing on their supremacy. Obviously he deserves to die.

The crowd at large isn't privy to all that's taken place behind the scenes. So when Jesus reveals the leaders' lethal motives, some think he's gone berserk (v. 20). The local residents, however, know the inside scoop, and they can't believe the Jewish leaders are letting Jesus speak like this right out in the open (v. 26). This brings up an important point. In this crowd there are mixed opinions about Jesus (cf. vv. 40-43). Some think he is God's gift to men (literally). Others think he is hell on wheels. Not only is there a mixed opinion about him, there are lots of different issues being raised. For example, they argue about his academic credentials (vv. 15-16), whether he has broken the law (vv. 19-24), and his roots (v. 27,42-43). Standing on the edge of this crowd is like watching three tennis games on a single court all at once. It tends to make one dizzy. So much is happening, and it's happening so fast.

Let's push pause, step back, and analyze what's going on. Two things emerge. First, there is a recurring refrain in this text. They keep trying to arrest him (vv. 30,32,44-46), but they can't get at him. Why? John's explanation is that it was not yet Jesus' time. God had other plans, so there was some kind of protective "force field" around him. The explanation of the temple guards is somewhat different (although not contradictory). They said, "No one ever taught like he did." Jesus' very words kept them at bay. The sheer force of his teachings stymied all opposition.

The second thing to emerge is one of those striking statements of Jesus, "If anyone is thirsty, let him come to me and drink" (v. 37). This is important at several levels. For starters, Jesus utters this against the backdrop of the Feast of Tabernacles. One of the important elements of this feast was the daily parade from the temple, to the pool of Siloam. The priest carried a golden pitcher, retrieved some water and poured it out at the base of the altar. There's gobs of symbolism here. The bottom line is that Jesus is claiming to fulfill the very feast they were celebrating. No matter where you stand, this is a bodacious declaration. More than that, this claim stands at the very center of the argument. While many issues were bantered about, the basic argument is over the person of Jesus — who he is, where he comes from, what he does. Jesus, in a parched and barren land, cries out, "I'll tell you who I am . . . I am the water of life and the only one who can slake your spiritual thirst." Without apology he makes the boldest of claims.

Finally, John, in a parenthetical explanation, interprets Jesus' words. He said this water, poured into and gushing out of a believer's life, is the Holy Spirit. The argument about Jesus' identity still rages. There are still many opinions about him. But for those of us who have believed in his words, who have dared to accept his claims, this towering truth stands above all petty squabbles: Jesus is the water of life. Through his Spirit, poured into our hearts, we see clearly who he is. It is this Holy Spirit geyser that settles the argument once and for all.

Further Reading: John 7:14-44.

Ponderable Questions: In this argument, what claims does Jesus make for himself? How would those have played with the Pharisees of his day? How would they play today if a university professor made such claims on his campus? Why should we believe Jesus? How does the Holy Spirit confirm these claims? How is this like water in our lives?

Considerations for Prayer: Holy Spirit, show yourself to be water in my life to cleanse, nourish, refresh, and heal.

Sinner in the Hand of an Angry Mob

{John 8:3-7; § 97}

The teachers of the law and the Pharisees brought in a woman caught in adultery. They made her stand before the group and said to Jesus, "Teacher, this woman was caught in the act of adultery. In the Law Moses commanded us to stone such women. Now what do you say?" They were using this question as a trap, in order to have a basis for accusing him. But Jesus bent down and started to write on the ground with his finger. When they kept on questioning him, he straightened up and said to them, "If any one of you is without sin, let him be the first to throw a stone at her."

This hot-blooded woman was caught red-handed. In those predawn moments she was ripped from the arms of her illicit lover. She frantically dressed while being dragged from her bed and paraded through the streets of Jerusalem. By the time she arrived at the temple, the sun was up and class was in session. Jesus had already assembled a group of eager students. She was thrown down in their midst. There she lay on the cold stone pavement trying to cover her bare thigh. Her hair was disheveled, her eyes wide and wild with fear and shame. Oh, the shame! Even the silent stones of the stately temple seemed to mock her as a shameless whore.

Jesus appears disinterested in all this messy business. The ringleaders of this tawdry sting point disparagingly at her and shout hate-filled slogans from the law. The Master stoops, quietly scribbling something in the sand. This self-appointed posse presses him for an answer. "Look, we know she's guilty, we saw her with our own eyes! What does the law say we should do?!" Jesus stands slowly and deliberately, "Well," he says, "the law commands you to stone her . . . so go ahead. Stone her." These words must have shot through her like and electric jolt. "But," he continues, "before you do, be sure that you have no guilt in this."

Before continuing with the story, a bit of background is in order. For an execution to be legal, there had to be witnesses. These witnesses could have no ulterior motives (such as extortion or involvement in the crime). Therefore, these witnesses are actually illegal witnesses at three levels. First, they are only interested in this woman's crime as a way of getting at Jesus. It is him they're after, not her. Second, she was likely set up. After all, how else does one become an eyewitness to adultery? These peeping Thomases are scandalous. Third, if they did, in fact, entrap her, then they could have stopped her before she committed the act. They knowingly let it go on, merely to get at Jesus. This whole business is rather messy.

Jesus says, "Let him who is without sin cast the first stone." Their eyes fall to the ground. One by one their stones do as well. Beginning with those most tempered by wisdom, they drop their charges and leave. Dull thuds shatter the silence, slowly at first, then increasing like popcorn. Finally Jesus is left alone with this woman. His silent students stare from the perimeter with wonder. He says, "Woman, who accuses you now?" "No one," she replies. "Then neither do I. But go and sin no more."

Perhaps the reason the church clings so tenaciously to this text is that it engulfs so many of us. Some encounter Christ with sexual sins, others with equally flagrant transgressions. All of us, however, come broken and shamed. For many the stoning would be a merciful release. But beyond belief, Jesus dismantles the accusers and dismisses the charges. The legal penalty he took upon himself. For our part, we get up, brush ourselves off, and walk away free — not free to live our lives, but free to transform them. Free, indeed, to die to the sin that entrapped us and live to the one who rescued us.

Further Reading: Galatians 5:13-18.

Ponderable Questions: Define grace. Have you really applied that definition to your own life? If Jesus does not condemn us, who are these people in the circle? Could you even be one of them? What do you think Jesus would say to sinners today? How does that differ from what preachers often say?

Considerations for Prayer: Tie a string to your watch or purse today. Each time you look at it thank God for the forgiveness and freedom you have in Christ.

Outrageous Claims of Christ – Part 2

{John 8:12-59; § 98-99}

v. 12: "I am the light of the world."

v. 24: "If you do not believe that I am the one I claim to be, you will indeed die in your sins."

v. 28: "When you have lifted up the Son of Man, then you will know that I am the one I claim to be."

v. 32: "Then you will know the truth, and the truth will set you free."

v. 46: "Can any of you prove me guilty of sin?"

v. 58: "I tell you the truth," Jesus answered, "before Abraham was born, I am!"

Arguments often degenerate into name-calling. This is a prime example. It began back in John 7 when Jesus arrived at the Feast of Tabernacles. Now, three and a half days later, on the last day of the feast, their differences have escalated into a full-scale fracas. Jesus stands in the temple, making outrageous claims. Some believe him, others doubt, still others are adamantly opposed. As a result, this lively discussion seems schizophrenic. Sometimes Jesus will talk tenderly, as he would to disciples. Then he turns right around and angrily assaults the crowd. This makes no sense until one sees the crowd as a hybrid of faith and doubt, of admiration and antagonism. As always, Jesus stands in the center, delighting some, shocking all.

He makes a number of claims that are outrageous! Really, if anyone else said such things, they would be offered a nice white jacket with really long sleeves. Here he is, a "hick" from Galilee, that claims to be the light of the world (v. 12). This must have sounded strange in the extreme coming from such a backwoods commoner. Then he threatened them with hell if they didn't follow him (v. 24). But if they did follow him, he would be their national hero and deliver them from slavery to sin (v. 33-36). He says he can make good on his promise because he is the sinless Son of God (v. 46-47). In fact, he is Yahweh himself, right in their presence (v. 58)!

Now come on . . . put away the Sunday school curriculum for just a second and think realistically about this. Who in their right mind would believe such outrageous nonsense? Jesus sounds like a lunatic. Why? He says it's because we don't know the Father (v. 42)! We think we do because we have so skillfully painted our self-portraits and convinced ourselves they are divine. Our theological systems are mirror images of our own desires and dreams. Yet the one true God stands outside our imaginations as a self-existing reality, demanding to be reckoned with. Jesus, God's envoy, would rather appear insane than condescend to our constricting standards of what he's supposed to be.

The primary question is not "What is God like?" Rather, it is, "Who is able to adequately describe him?" Such a person would, indeed, appear insane on our level. Thus Jesus' radical claims do not necessarily disqualify him from deity. So what one must decide is whether Jesus' claims are believable, not whether they are reasonable. Granted, this will take a massive act of evidence. That is precisely what he pointed to in verse 28, "When you have lifted up the Son of Man," he says, "then you will know that I am the one I claim to be and that I do nothing on my own but speak just what the Father has taught me." Obviously the term "lifted up" refers to the crucifixion. In John's writing, however, it also includes the resurrection and ascension. The three are pulled together into one package. Since no one was convinced of Christ's claims merely by his execution, he must have in mind his impending exaltation. Granted, it's been a long time in coming, but when Jesus' enemies see him return on the clouds of heaven, there will be no doubt that they radically misunderstood his identity. His forthcoming return will be sufficient evidence for all.

As for the resurrection, while it didn't do much for his enemies, it is the centerpiece of discipleship. For those inclined to believe, this event is our cornerstone of faith. It makes sense of who Jesus is and validates all his radical claims. His insane demands suddenly make sense. This peasant from Palestine can, in fact, introduce us to God. This wild-eyed wanderer is actually the very vision of Yahweh. In a sense, he is as foreign to the church as he is to his enemies. They portrayed him as insane, we have pictured him as domesticated. Both will be sorely surprised. He is neither tame nor reasonable. He is wild and demanding, extreme and dangerous — not the kind of creature you casually walk on a leash.

Further Reading: John 8:12-59; "Jesus' Claims to Deity" — available in electronic form from College Press.

Ponderable Questions: Go back through the claims Jesus made in this text, pretending he is not divine. How would he look? Read them again, assuming he is divine. How does he look now? Read through Ephesians 1:3-14 listing all the blessings we have in Christ.

Considerations for Prayer: Revisit the lists in John 8 and Ephesians 1. Praise God for all we have in Christ.

Blind Man's Bluff

{John 9:1-7; § 100}

As he went along, he saw a man blind from birth. His disciples asked him, "Rabbi, who sinned, this man or his parents, that he was born blind?" "Neither this man nor his parents sinned," said Jesus, "but this happened so that the work of God might be displayed in his life. As long as it is day, we must do the work of him who sent me. Night is coming, when no one can work. While I am in the world, I am the light of the world." Having said this, he spit on the ground, made some mud with the saliva, and put it on the man's eyes. "Go," he told him, "wash in the Pool of Siloam" (this word means Sent). So the man went and washed, and came home seeing.

As Jesus and his disciples leave the temple they run across a blind man. Nothing so unusual about that in a third-world country. There are a couple of assumptions that we might make about this man. First, being blind in the vicinity of the temple almost certainly made him a beggar. There were lots of people with various infirmities that clustered about the temple gates. They held out their hands and pleaded for alms, and many pious worshipers obliged. They were feeling religious, and most had money to spare on sacrifices. The temple was a strategic place for beggars. Second, we might assume that this man was sharp. He clearly knew who Jesus was merely by his voice (cf. v. 11), and he holds his ground against the Pharisees when they pummel him with questions about the healing (vv. 16-17,24-34). He is blind, but he is far from stupid. He has listened well to the theological debates that pass in and out of these sacred precincts. Suddenly he finds himself in the middle of one.

The disciples ask Jesus who was responsible for this pathetic tragedy. Is God punishing him for some sin he committed? Or are his parents villains? These questions sound shocking since we don't share the Jewish ideology of the disciples. They were taught growing up that if a man sinned, his children might be smitten by God. Where would they get such a notion?! Actually, it comes from the Ten Commandments (Exod 20:5). God promised to punish a man's family down to the third and fourth generation. The reason this sounds so foreign to us is because we have been weaned on God's gracious new covenant (cf. Jer 31:29-34).

According to the disciples, the first possibility is that the parents sinned. The second possibility is that the blind man sinned. Considering, however, that he was born blind, his sin would have to have been in utero! Surprisingly, Jews did, in fact, believe that a child could sin in the womb. According to Genesis 25:22-26, some Rabbis taught that Jacob attempted to kill Esau. These two possibilities may seem strange. Perhaps that's because the problem of evil in this world is so vexing. How can we reconcile congenital blindness with a loving God? Jesus offers a third solution: "This happened so that the work of God might be displayed in his life."

Now that's shocking! Would God actually cause a man to be born blind so that in his later adult years God could glorify himself by healing him?! Is that really kindness?! Perhaps we need to be reminded of Romans 9:20-23. We don't have the right or the ability to critique the work of God. If the potter wants to make a lump of clay into a blind man, he certainly can. Call God what you will as long as you call him sovereign Lord. At the same time, Jesus' words do *not* necessarily mean that God created him blind for the *purpose* of glorifying himself. They may mean nothing more than the blindness would *result* in God's glory. That, in fact, fits the tenor of the passage better.

The disciples want to theologize about the man's condition. Jesus appears to bypass the question entirely in order to get at the need. It is as if he is saying, "Forget about whose fault it is! Let's do something about it!" He puts mud on the man's eyes and sends him off to Siloam. This healing is highly charged with symbolism. (1) A blind man meets the light of the world. (2) "Siloam" means "sent." Thus he was sent to "sent" to wash. (3) After washing with water he could see once more. Sound familiar? Somehow this story transcends a blind beggar. Look closely at the text and you'll see yourself. His story echoes our own. For like him, we were sent to wash and having washed, we see. We too were blind but have encountered the light of life. An encounter with Christ births Amazing Grace.

Further Reading: John 9:1-41.

Ponderable Questions: How is this man's story similar to your own conversion? Think through Ephesians 1:15-23 in relationship to John 9. Memorize Ephesians 1:18-19b. If Jesus is so good, why did he arouse such opposition? Why does he often today?

Considerations for Prayer: Sing "Amazing Grace."

45 The Good Shepherd 45

{John 10:10-14; § 101}

> The thief comes only to steal and kill and destroy; I have come that they may have life, and have it to the full. I am the good shepherd. The good shepherd lays down his life for the sheep. The hired hand is not the shepherd who owns the sheep. So when he sees the wolf coming, he abandons the sheep and runs away. Then the wolf attacks the flock and scatters it. The man runs away because he is a hired hand and cares nothing for the sheep. I am the good shepherd; I know my sheep and my sheep know me.

The good shepherd offers life to the full. What precisely does this mean? To begin with, let's consider what it does *not* mean. The wise king Solomon, a type of Christ himself, looked for life and came up empty. Ecclesiastes records his experiments with wine, women, wealth, and work. These God-given gifts, outside his providence, suck the marrow from the meaning of life. In his sunset years, Solomon confesses that he had it all, yet nothing mattered. What's worse is that in pursuing life, he lost it. That which was supposed to bring him joy was the very vortex that created the vacuum.

Solomon concluded that life *under the sun* was meaningless. Jesus claims that life *in the Son* is abundant. The thief comes to steal, kill, and destroy (v. 10). Jesus, in contrast, does not rob the sheeppen, rather, he feeds the sheep. He doesn't kill the sheep, rather he sacrifices himself on their behalf. And instead of destroying them, he builds them up. Therein lies life. *He* is our life, not the trinkets we imagine he offers. We often look for significance and pleasure in Solomon's experiments. Jesus calls us to come to him, and he alone will be our abundant life. He will be our wealth, our celebration, our satisfaction. When we take him at his word, when we follow by faith, when we submit to the shepherd, something mysterious and wonderful happens. As we desire nothing but Christ, as we pursue him alone, his presence in us infuses meaning into all other activities of life. Suddenly the affairs we necessarily find ourselves enmeshed in become abundant through Jesus. The former failed experiments with work, wine, women, and wealth are transformed into worship of the highest sort. When he is our center, the periphery is beautiful. Life in Christ becomes a scenic tour of Eden. To breathe is worship; to walk is dance; to sleep is Sabbath; to pray is communion; to love is celebration.

This can hardly be construed as some naive utopian dream. Jesus' words are forged within the angry conflict with his would-be assassins. Twice he claims to be the good shepherd. Both times he chases it with this explanation: The good shepherd lays down his life for the sheep. Abundant life is not oblivious to the terrors of opposition and suffering. Abundant life is the way of the cross, intimately acquainted with the *Via Dolorosa*. This life is *his* life. He laid it down so that we could take it up, experience it, be enveloped by it. His life does not skirt the boundaries of suffering. Rather, like a penetrating laser, his abundant life permeates even the darkest night of the soul. His life infuses and transforms; it infiltrates and dominates. It is revolutionary and sanguine, even violently jubilant. Life in Jesus is simply outrageous.

Further Reading: John 10:1-18; Ezekiel 34:1-31.

Ponderable Questions: What prompted Jesus to make these statements? How is this situation relevant to the prophecy of Ezekiel 34? How do religious systems rob people of life? How does Jesus infuse our existence with life to the full? What characteristics of a shepherd does Jesus share?

Considerations for Prayer: "Lord, make my life extraordinary."

The Sending of a New Sanhedrin

46

{Luke 10:1-2,17-21; § 102}

After this the Lord appointed seventy-two others and sent them two by two ahead of him to every town and place where he was about to go. He told them, "The harvest is plentiful, but the workers are few. Ask the Lord of the harvest, therefore, to send out workers into his harvest field. . . . The seventy-two returned with joy and said, "Lord, even the demons submit to us in your name." He replied, "I saw Satan fall like lightning from heaven. I have given you authority to trample on snakes and scorpions and to overcome all the power of the enemy; nothing will harm you. However, do not rejoice that the spirits submit to you, but rejoice that your names are written in heaven." At that time Jesus, full of joy through the Holy Spirit, said, "I praise you, Father, Lord of heaven and earth, because you have hidden these things from the wise and learned, and revealed them to little children. Yes, Father, for this was your good pleasure.

Satan falling from heaven, demons scurrying, snakes and scorpions being trampled . . . What fun! Joy is, in fact, one of the choral refrains of this text. The 72 return with joy (v. 17), Jesus is full of joy in the Holy Spirit (v. 21), and even God has "good pleasure" (v. 21). It's a strike-up-the-band kind of a passage. Sometimes, however, the 72 celebrate for the wrong reasons. This merits a closer look. We'll need to return to Jerusalem to get a running start at this text.

Feathers flew at the Feast of Tabernacles. After the dust settled, lots of good people ran after Jesus. They are ready to throw their support behind this most likely candidate for king. Jesus looks over the troops and selects 72 to be heralds of the soon-coming kingdom. He pairs them off and sends them out. The fields are white, and their hearts are red-hot. Their healings and exorcisms blaze a trail for Jesus' tour. All Judea is abuzz. In fact, the unseen spirit world is shaken as well.

The 72 share their extraordinary stories of how the incoming kingdom toppled the entrenched powers of evil. Jesus concurs, "Yes, I saw Satan fall like lightning." Now, there are two things about this verse we should see. First, the image of lightning, for us, indicates speed. In the Bible, however, it almost exclusively refers to something that is seen widely. After all, when lightning strikes, how can anyone miss it? We tend to turn to the person next to us and say, "Did you see that?!" They reply, "Duh!" So it was with Satan falling. It was seen all over the place. That brings up a second point. The word "I saw" in Greek is spelled exactly like the word "they saw." In other words, the verse could just as easily say, "The demons saw Satan falling everywhere." In some ways that makes even more sense. Everywhere these preachers went, the work of Satan was undone and his underlings overwhelmed. No wonder these guys were so jazzed. They were on the cutting edge of the Devil's demise!

Jesus rejoices at this as well. However, he cautions them to keep the right focus. Power encounters may be wonderful and exhilarating, but they are not best. What is more incredible and exciting is the fact that our names are inscribed in heaven. Indeed, it is a joyous thing for evil to be thwarted. Greater still is to be accepted by God. The icing on the cake is this, God has accepted the weak things of this world as instruments for demonic demolition. We are but children, yet used to trample snakes and scorpions. We rejoice, therefore, in God's greatness, not ours. We celebrate his work in us, not our work for him.

Further Reading: Luke 10:1-23; 2 Corinthians 5:11-21.

Ponderable Questions: To the best of your ability, describe the spiritual battle we're in. Do you have a sense either personally or in your church, that you are at war? How do we wage this war? If we are Christ's delegates, what kind of authority has he given us to carry out his work?

Considerations for Prayer: Lord, enlist me in your army; sustain me with your authority.

47 The "Good" Samaritan 47

{Luke 10:25-31,36-37; § 103}

On one occasion an expert in the law stood up to test Jesus. "Teacher," he asked, "what must I do to inherit eternal life?" "What is written in the Law?" he replied. "How do you read it?" He answered: "'Love the Lord your God with all your heart and with all your soul and with all your strength and with all your mind'; and, 'Love your neighbor as yourself.'" "You have answered correctly," Jesus replied. "Do this and you will live." But he wanted to justify himself, so he asked Jesus, "And who is my neighbor?" In reply Jesus said: "A man was going down from Jerusalem to Jericho, when he fell into the hands of robbers. They stripped him of his clothes, beat him and went away, leaving him half dead. . . . "Which of these three do you think was a neighbor to the man who fell into the hands of robbers?" The expert in the law replied, "The one who had mercy on him." Jesus told him, "Go and do likewise."

Del was a student in the college where I teach and a member of a traveling music group that performed in churches on the weekends. It was half ministry and half recruitment. Families of the congregation would host the kids after each performance. Some of the homes were opulent, others quite modest. One particular evening, this young man stayed with a family that was obviously not well-off. Sitting around the dinner table, he asked the man of the house what he did for a living. This father's face beamed, "Well, I just got a new job . . . Before that," he said, "I was out of work for more than two years." Del replied, "That must have been tough. I bet the church helped out though." The man hung his head, and without any bitterness, told this story: "Actually, they didn't. We asked for help but they were in the middle of a building campaign and said there just weren't any extra funds. It was bad, really bad. I remember the night we were sitting down at our kitchen table for our last meal. We had opened a can of green beans. We didn't even heat them up because our power had been shut off. Just as we were praying for the meal we hear a loud knock at the door. When I opened the door, there stood my neighbor. What you must understand is that you wouldn't like my neighbors much. They drink all the time and leave beer bottles lying around. They peel rubber up and down the street. We're afraid even to let our kids play in the yard. But there he stood with an electrical cord in his hand that stretched over from his house. When I asked him what he was doing, he awkwardly shuffled his feet and shoved the cord in my hand. He said gruffly, 'Well, you can't live without power!' And he left."

This story is uncomfortable for the church. We're not used to surly neighbors wearing white hats. It's the godly that are supposed to come to the rescue, not drunken neighbors. The questions this raises are no less difficult than the ones Jesus' story raised. When the lawyer asked, "What must I do to be saved?" he was clearly after self justification. So are we. He was able to answer his own question about keeping the commandments. So are we. He was even able to differentiate between the core commands of love and the superfluous rituals of his religious code. So are we. Yet he still felt a need to narrow the field. He needed a smaller target for the recipients of his love. So do we.

There are two words he could have used for "neighbor." The first simply means, "Those who live around you." He chose the second. It means, "Those whom you're next to." He wanted to restrict the recipients of his love to those he touched, not merely those who hovered about his home. Jesus said through this story, "You're correct; your 'neighbor' is the one you touch — everyone you touch." When we pass someone on the road, when we bump into a total stranger at the market, when we casually contact a teller or a clerk, a child, or a homeless person, these individuals become our neighbors through human contact. At this point we must revisit the original question the lawyer asked: "What must I do to be saved?" Jesus' response boils down to this: *To be saved* you must extend to those you encounter the kindness, attention, and resources they need.

This story is terribly popular in children's church because we imagine that it will encourage the kiddos to be civil. But the minute they start taking Jesus' advice, most parents strenuously demand that they be reasonable. "Don't talk to strangers," they say. "Don't pick up hitchhikers." "Don't be gullible with charity!" This all makes sense — too much sense. It contradicts Jesus' advice to a very reasonable religious leader. This story is outrageous and unrealistic. It is dangerous advice and a preposterous demand. If the church actually chose to live like this, Christians would be robbed, taken advantage of, and ridiculed — and what a marvelous place this world would be.

Further Reading: Galatians 6:9-10; Hebrews 13:1-3.

Ponderable Questions: How does Paul answer the question, "What must I do to be saved?" How does this relate to what Jesus says here? Do you think Jesus' teaching here is reasonable? Safe? Necessary? What could it cost you to live like this? What potential benefits does it hold?

Considerations for Prayer: Invite the Holy Spirit to convict you to be a person of dangerous and costly compassion.

48 Only One Thing Is Needed 48

{Luke 10:38-42; § 104}

As Jesus and his disciples were on their way, he came to a village where a woman named Martha opened her home to him. She had a sister called Mary, who sat at the Lord's feet listening to what he said. But Martha was distracted by all the preparations that had to be made. She came to him and asked, "Lord, don't you care that my sister has left me to do the work by myself? Tell her to help me!" "Martha, Martha," the Lord answered, "you are worried and upset about many things, but only one thing is needed. Mary has chosen what is better, and it will not be taken away from her."

She was the model woman: a gracious host, a domestic dynamo, a real servant heart. When Martha heard that Jesus was in the area, she insisted on hosting him for dinner. She and her sister Mary went to work. They scampered off to the market to purchase everything they would need for an impressive sit-down meal for thirteen or more men. Any woman can tell you this is no easy task. First one needs to plan the menu and calculate the correct portions. There are *hors d'oeuvres*, side dishes, sauces, desserts, bread, salad, and wine. This sort of thing doesn't just fall together, you know! One must decide on place settings and seating arrangements, music and lighting. The cooking must be meticulously planned, timed, and carefully executed. Then there is the whole preparatory housecleaning before the guests arrive. Perhaps hardest of all are the plastic smile and cultured conversations one must produce while spinning a dozen plates or more for the guests. Martha knew well what it took to pull off a dinner party. But it was well worth it, for she knew well what kind of honor Jesus deserved.

After frantic preparations, the day finally arrived. The guests filed in and filled the room with laughter, jokes, and stories. The kitchen kicked into high gear. The guests were treated like royalty. Plates of sumptuous food were presented on platters. The appropriate articulation of "ooohs," "aaaaahs," and "mmmmms" rewarded Martha for all her hard work. The best was yet to come. Jesus began to teach. Martha had provided the setting. It was all so satisfying. While she shuttled between the kitchen and the dining hall, she caught snippets of his wisdom on the fly.

It was perfect . . . except for one thing. When Jesus began to lecture, Mary took a seat. She sat there wide-eyed, oblivious to the obligations she was neglecting. It was outrageous! She abandoned Martha to do the work herself. What's worse, she was sitting where she didn't belong. A woman student?! It was presumptuous, irresponsible, and out of place. With each trip into the banquet hall Martha glared at Mary, trying to catch her eye and rebuke her with a glance. Mary was riveted to Jesus. Martha got angrier and angrier, until finally she erupted.

"Jesus, Mary has abandoned me to do all this work alone. Tell her to do her fair share!" Now that is a reasonable request if there ever was one. You would expect, after all, for Jesus to support a Judeo-Christian work ethic. He does not. Rather, he rebukes Martha. "Martha, Martha, you are upset and agitated about too many things." Now isn't that an appropriate headline for an American biography?! We've got soccer games and appointments, work-out schedules and taxes, e-mail and bills. It all seems so significant. Our Day-Timers loom large over our daily grind. It is easy enough to look back at Martha and see how foolish she was. She had God-Incarnate in her living room, and she was worried about tea and crumpets! Yet stand beside her for a millisecond and you will recognize the resemblance. What we fret over is no more significant. Indeed, we too have intimate access to God that we neglect for trifles. We tinker at our worship and work at our worry. We scurry instead of dance, labor instead of listen, we plan instead of adore. How appropriate Jesus' words still are, "Mary has chosen the better, and it will not be taken away from her."

Dear Christian Martha, Jesus never asked for a meal; he craves a companion. He's not impressed with your labor but with your obedience. He would rather have your ear than your programs, your heart than your hands. Certainly we're not called to sedentary discipleship. But the work we do must come from the overflow of being at his feet. Our work begins with Sabbath; our labor is an overflow of listening.

Further Reading: Revelation 2:1-7.

Ponderable Questions: Why is working hard for Jesus sometimes so wrong? Have you ever been burned out in service for the church? Describe what that's like and how one recaptures that "first love." Are you more like Mary or Martha? Why?

Considerations for Prayer: Mark out some time in your schedule today that you can just be with Jesus and rekindle your love for him. Tell him how much you've missed him.

How to Pray with Persistence

{Luke 11:1-2a,9-13; § 105}

One day Jesus was praying in a certain place. When he finished, one of his disciples said to him, "Lord, teach us to pray, just as John taught his disciples." He said to them, "When you pray, say: 'Father, hallowed be your name . . .' So I say to you: Ask and it will be given to you; seek and you will find; knock and the door will be opened to you. For everyone who asks receives; he who seeks finds; and to him who knocks, the door will be opened. Which of you fathers, if your son asks for a fish, will give him a snake instead? Or if he asks for an egg, will give him a scorpion? If you then, though you are evil, know how to give good gifts to your children, how much more will your Father in heaven give the Holy Spirit to those who ask him!"

Books on prayer are about as common as diet plans and exercise videos, and for the same reason — people are fat and lazy. They are looking for a quick fix to a deeply ingrained problem. They want a magical formula, a wand to wave that won't demand too much of a change. This is a very old quest. Jesus' own disciples, like so many other students, asked for guidance in this spiritual discipline of prayer.

Jesus offers them what we have labeled "The Lord's Prayer." On the surface it looks like a formula, a set of phrases to string together in order to pray properly. In some ways it works well as a kind of model prayer. But deeper than the words themselves, Jesus is opening up a new kind of relationship with God. It is this relationship, not the formula, that is the foundation of prayer.

The whole of the Lord's prayer deserves attention which it will not receive here. For our purposes, we are interested only in the first phrase, "Our Father in heaven." This is revolutionary! The Jews were familiar with the concept of God as father of their nation. But no other rabbi conceived of God as "Abba." To think of God as the progenitor of a people is one thing. To adopt him as a personal father is another altogether! This new relationship with Yahweh is no less sacred, for his name is still holy. It does, however, open up an unprecedented opportunity for intimacy with God. The Holy of Holies and the hierarchy of priests become irrelevant. We peons become princes with access to the throne. More than that, through the Holy Spirit (v. 13) we come boldly. Now there is a bizarre thought! We would be fools to come flippantly or irreverently. Nonetheless, because we come as children, we come with confidence. That is the purpose of Jesus' parable in verses 5-8. We can "pester" God with our petitions as persistently as we would knock on the door of our next-door neighbor at midnight. Now, one would assume that you need a good reason to wake up a friend at midnight. But with just cause you can bang away because of your relationship. So too with God: We can bring our needs to him with confidence and persistence as children do with a loving father.

In fact, Jesus bids us "ask, seek, knock." Why? Precisely because we are children of a loving father. If we, as earthly parents, know how to delight our children by supplying their needs, how much more does God know about showering blessings on us?! Let's not get distracted here. Jesus is obviously not talking about creating spiritual spoiled brats through materialistic indulgence. In fact, verse 13 identifies the greatest gift God desires to give: The Holy Spirit! The point is not how much we can accumulate if we pester God. It is this: The foundation of prayer is relationship, not program. If you don't pray as you ought, it is not because you've not been properly taught the correct formula, it is because you've not been properly introduced to your heavenly Father. Jesus said, "I am the way, the truth and the life. No one comes to the Father except through me" (John 14:6). Don't work at prayer; work at the relationship. Then the conversation will flow freely.

Further Reading: Luke 11:1-13; 18:1-14; John 14:12-20; "Prayer" — available in electronic form from College Press.

Ponderable Questions: Why is the Holy Spirit such an integral part of these prayer texts? How would our prayers be different if we worked at the relational aspect of our conversations with God? How would it alter what we say to God and what we ask from him? Pay attention to your own prayers this week, as well as those at corporate worship. How much is about relationship and how much is merely a shopping list?

Considerations for Prayer: Ask Abba to give you his Holy Spirit.

Words We Refuse to Believe

{Luke 12:13-15,32-34; § 108b}

Someone in the crowd said to him, "Teacher, tell my brother to divide the inheritance with me." Jesus replied, "Man, who appointed me a judge or an arbiter between you?" Then he said to them, "Watch out! Be on your guard against all kinds of greed; a man's life does not consist in the abundance of his possessions. . . . Do not be afraid, little flock, for your Father has been pleased to give you the kingdom. Sell your possessions and give to the poor. Provide purses for yourselves that will not wear out, a treasure in heaven that will not be exhausted, where no thief comes near and no moth destroys. For where your treasure is, there your heart will be also."

We all like to pretend that we believe Jesus. We imagine that he is rather like us. For if we can convince ourselves of this, then we can feel secure, almost smug, in our salvation. The problem is that this security comes with a price. That is, we must decimate a number of his statements in order to whittle them down to our size. Our present text is a case in point.

Jesus' words, taken literally, are too much to handle. They must be manhandled if they are to be properly managed. It began when a man approached Jesus with a rather bold request: "Jesus, tell my brother to give me my fair share of the inheritance." While Jesus is not a legal judge, it was not uncommon for respected rabbi's to arbitrate between individuals, especially their own disciples. In a way this is quite a heady compliment for Jesus. If he takes it up, however, it will send his ministry into a tailspin. He didn't come to settle legal disputes between men but to settle the legal dispute God has with sin.

He sends the man away empty handed but not before he gives him an earful. First he tells a parable about a rich man who continued to store his surplus into barns. The very day he finally felt satisfied with his social security, his soul was required at judgment. Of course, this illustration would be particularly poignant to this young man who just lost his wealthy father. Jesus' conclusion is simple: "This is how it will be with anyone who stores up things for himself but is not rich toward God."

This brings up a second point. If you spend all your time and energy preparing to meet God, who will watch over your portfolio? Jesus' answer is, "The very God you seek, and the only one truly able to offer you security." He uses familiar phrases in verses 22-32. They are snatched from the Sermon on the Mount (Matt. 6:21,25-34). Apparently this lesson on worry bears repeating. To live for luxury is to deny God's power to provide. Materialism is practical atheism, and to ignore the poor is blasphemous neglect.

Yet who actually believes this? Oh sure, there are some. I suppose the real question is "Do *you* believe this?" Don't answer with your lips; answer with your checkbook. Please don't misunderstand. This is not a tirade against insurance, IRAs, or bank accounts. It is, however, a clarion call for introspection. Do we really trust that God is an adequate provider? Is he sufficient for our needs and desires? It is no longer acceptable to sit in the lap of American luxury and to ignore the world's poor while pretending to be followers of Jesus.

In case you think you can have your cake and eat it, too, remember Jesus' words, "No man can serve two masters." Yes, he *was* talking about money! We may not be called to be paupers or ascetics. Nevertheless, we are called to eliminate the excessive baggage that reveals our unbelief. If Jesus is not our only treasure, then our inheritance is in jeopardy.

Further Reading: Luke 12:13-34; 16:19-31; Revelation 3:14-21.

Ponderable Questions: What are some of the spiritual dangers of being wealthy? In what ways is your wealth a hindrance to full discipleship of Jesus? What are some practical steps we could take to bring our finances under the Lordship of Christ?

Considerations for Prayer: Lay your checkbook open on the table and pray through the register. Repent for selfishness, thank God for blessings, ask for his priorities to be revealed.

51 A New Kind of Rest 51

{Luke 13:10-17; § 110}

On a Sabbath Jesus was teaching in one of the synagogues, and a woman was there who had been crippled by a spirit for eighteen years. She was bent over and could not straighten up at all. When Jesus saw her, he called her forward and said to her, "Woman, you are set free from your infirmity." Then he put his hands on her, and immediately she straightened up and praised God. Indignant because Jesus had healed on the Sabbath, the synagogue ruler said to the people, "There are six days for work. So come and be healed on those days, not on the Sabbath." The Lord answered him, "You hypocrites! Doesn't each of you on the Sabbath untie his ox or donkey from the stall and lead it out to give it water? Then should not this woman, a daughter of Abraham, whom Satan has kept bound for eighteen long years, be set free on the Sabbath day from what bound her?" When he said this, all his opponents were humiliated, but the people were delighted with all the wonderful things he was doing.

The rules were very clear. According to the oral traditions of Jesus' day, now recorded in the Mishna, one could only provide life-saving medical treatment on the Sabbath. Anything more was considered work. The idea was simple: God said not to work, but saving a life is more important than keeping that command. Thus God would want you to work to save a life, even if it would break a Sabbath ordinance.

No one is arguing that this woman's situation was pathetic. She had been oppressed by a demon for eighteen years! This devilish imp crippled her with something like osteoporosis. It was just horrible. The point of the Pharisees, however, was that if she had been in that condition for 18 years, what is another few hours going to hurt? They weren't against the healing, they were against the timing. According to their logic, this all makes sense.

Jesus' logic is quite different. Instead of prioritizing religious ritual, he prioritizes people. When the synagogue ruler rebuked him, Jesus lashed back. "You hypocrite," he said, "You will take care of your donkey on the Sabbath, but not this daughter of Abraham?!" Jesus isn't even gentle. This is one thing that makes his blood boil. In fact, one of the only times the Bible says Jesus got angry was over this very issue back in Mark 3:1-6. Same scene, same song, same conclusions, only instead of a woman bowed double, it was a man with a withered hand. Moreover, he will do it again with a man suffering from dropsy (Luke 14:1-6).

This appears to be a consistent battle waged between Jesus' system of ethics and the Pharisees'. All four Gospel writers recorded multiple Sabbath controversies (Matt. 12:1-8,9-14; Mark 2:23-28; 3:1-6; Luke 6:1-5,6-11; 13:10-17; 14:1-6; John 5:10-18; 7:21-24; 9:1-17). These represent no less than seven separate healings. In other words, this sort of thing happened a *lot*. What, pray tell, does this mean? Well, for one thing, it means that Jesus is not offering an addendum to a fairly satisfactory religious system. Rather, he is offering an alternative morality. He concentrates on needs of people rather than the rules of God. This is not to say that God's decrees are irrelevant. By no means! It is to say that their purpose is to heal people, not to promote an ecclesiastical hierarchy. If the truth be told, God cares little about church polity in deference for the Church.

An honest look would probably betray how close we are to this synagogue ruler and how far from Jesus. Consider the last line of this story. "His opponents were humiliated, but the people were delighted with all the wonderful things he was doing." True Christianity is generally offensive to religious people but a delight to the downtrodden. If your own assembly is comfortable for religious people, then it is likely a place where Jesus' presence would be uncomfortable.

Further Reading: Matthew 12:1-8,9-14; Mark 2:23-28; 3:1-6; Luke 6:1-5,6-11; 13:10-17; 14:1-6; John 5:10-18; 7:21-24; 9:1-17.

Ponderable Questions: Based on these Sabbath controversies, try to formulate Jesus' view of the Sabbath. What does this reveal about Jesus' priority for people? If Jesus were to enter your church and do these same kinds of things, what problems would he cause? How can we imitate Jesus in his treatment of people, and what might that cost us?

Considerations for Prayer: Make a list before the Lord of all the downtrodden people who cross your path each week. Ask him what you should do for/with them.

Poachers, Beware!

{John 10:24-30; § 111}

The Jews gathered around him, saying, "How long will you keep us in suspense? If you are the Christ, tell us plainly." Jesus answered, "I did tell you, but you do not believe. The miracles I do in my Father's name speak for me, but you do not believe because you are not my sheep. My sheep listen to my voice; I know them, and they follow me. I give them eternal life, and they shall never perish; no one can snatch them out of my hand. My Father, who has given them to me, is greater than all; no one can snatch them out of my Father's hand. I and the Father are one."

Scott is a far cry from Jesus. One day, however, they looked just alike. I was a boy of slight build, meek and mild. One day at recess I got picked on by a bully. He promised me a good thrashing when school let out. I feared for my life when that odious bell rang, the harbinger of my impending demise. (To a second grader, such threats loom large.) Scott, my senior by two years, had heard about the threat and came to my rescue. I don't remember exactly the words exchanged that afternoon. But Scott assured him that should any bodily injury come to my person he would take it personally. No one was going to hurt his little brother! (Except him, of course.) I remember how secure I felt at the side of my hero. I felt bold and loved, protected and therefore confident. This ugly altercation was, to me, a beautiful moment.

That is exactly what Jesus is doing here. It is the Feast of Dedication, December A.D. 32. He is three months ahead of the cross and the friction is white-hot. Some of the Jewish leaders not only accost Jesus, but they try to intimidate his followers. Jesus' fraternal zeal is kindled. They threaten to steal his sheep. He replies, "Over my dead body!" Actually, it was more than that. For even his dead body would not allow the poachers entrance into the fold.

Many take this as a wonderful promise to Christians. Indeed, it is that. First and foremost, however, it is a very serious threat to the enemies of the flock. That, in part, is what makes it such a wonderful promise. It is not that Jesus tenderly coddles his sheep, but that he viciously threatens our enemies. This is a "make my day" kind of a text. Because of that, we stand with bold confidence that Jesus is our protector.

Many enemies would love to sink their teeth into the church. Jesus stands as a vigilant guard at the gate. As Paul says in Romans 8:37-39, "No, in all these things we are more than conquerors through him who loved us. For I am convinced that neither death nor life, neither angels nor demons, neither the present nor the future, nor any powers, neither height nor depth, nor anything else in all creation, will be able to separate us from the love of God that is in Christ Jesus our Lord."

There is no wolf crafty enough, no thief quick enough, no enemy strong enough, no devil fierce enough to sever us from the Savior. We heard his voice and followed him. Thus we became part of his flock. As such, we are eternally secure in Christ. Our loyalty to him is matched by his allegiance to us. Good Christian take heart. You have a living Lord who is a gentle shepherd and a fierce advocate. You need not fear for your soul. Jesus himself is watching over it.

Further Reading: 2 Thessalonians 3:3-5; "Eternal Security Worksheet" — available in electronic form from College Press.

Ponderable Questions: How does it make you feel that Jesus is viciously protective of you? As a sheep, what is your appropriate response to his protection? Why do we sometimes doubt our salvation? What can we do to remember and celebrate our security in Christ?

Considerations for Prayer: Praise God for his protection; pledge him your allegiance.

Encounters with Christ

The Later Perean Ministry

Go Tell That Fox

{Luke 13:31-33; § 113}

At that time some Pharisees came to Jesus and said to him, "Leave this place and go somewhere else. Herod wants to kill you." He replied, "Go tell that fox, 'I will drive out demons and heal people today and tomorrow, and on the third day I will reach my goal.' In any case, I must keep going today and tomorrow and the next day—for surely no prophet can die outside Jerusalem!

Herod is a mess! He already beheaded John because of a drunken promise to his sultry step-daughter. Now he's after Jesus! Why not? They both preach repentance, which irritated Herod. And both preached a coming-soon kingdom of the Jews that was in direct opposition to Herod's reign. It comes as no surprise that he was eager to see Jesus. After all, this public pest was attracting crowds that looked dangerously like a new revolutionary movement.

What comes as a surprise is that the *Pharisees* would try to protect Jesus from him. Granted, Herod was no friend of the Pharisees. He aligned himself with their antagonists, the Sadducees. Yet both of these groups had agreed that Jesus must die. So why warn him of Herod's designs? Most likely what is happening is not some tenderhearted Pharisees trying to save Jesus' neck. Rather, they are likely trying to lure him to Jerusalem. His current ministry in Perea is fabulously successful, and the Pharisees are losing ground. Their party would very much like to get him back in the capital city where they have the distinct advantage. A threat like this just might do the trick.

Jesus is hardly intimidated. In fact, when he calls Herod a fox, this metaphor does not primarily mean someone who is tricky, like it does for us. In biblical literature, a fox is a small, insignificant pest (cf. Neh. 4:3; S. of S. 2:15). Furthermore, Jesus uses the feminine form of the word. Not only is he calling Herod a fox, he is calling him a she-fox. Likely Jesus is referring to the fact that his wicked wife is the impetus behind his schemes.

Jesus' reply reveals Herod's true character. Then he turns on the Pharisees and reveals theirs when he says, "No prophet can die outside Jerusalem." It is almost as if he says, "You want me in Jerusalem to execute me . . . you will get your wish, but only when I'm ready." It is also telling that Jesus refers to his three days in the area. Any allusion to the death of Jesus is incomplete without some reference to the resurrection.

Once again, Jesus' life is a model for ours. Following Jesus hardly means that all opposition will turn tail and run. Rather, the fact that we are his disciples is a pretty good indication that tensions will escalate. Ours is not to run and hide. Because we believe in a sovereign God with a perfect plan and impeccable timing, we can stay the course. This doesn't mean we avoid tribulation. After all, Jesus did still wind up on a cross in Jerusalem. It does mean, however, that we stand boldly in the face of intimidation and threats. One of the key characteristics of an encounter with Christ is a clarity of purpose. Good Christian, stay the course.

Further Reading: Acts 4:1-21.

Ponderable Questions: What is an appropriate Christian response to secular persecution? Have you experienced this in your life? What were the results? What role does the Holy Spirit play in helping us imitate the boldness of Jesus?

Considerations for Prayer: Pray for the persecuted church around the world.

Jesus' Table Manners with the Pharisees

{Luke 14:7-11; § 114}

When he noticed how the guests picked the places of honor at the table, he told them this parable: "When someone invites you to a wedding feast, do not take the place of honor, for a person more distinguished than you may have been invited. If so, the host who invited both of you will come and say to you, 'Give this man your seat.' Then, humiliated, you will have to take the least important place. But when you are invited, take the lowest place, so that when your host comes, he will say to you, 'Friend, move up to a better place.' Then you will be honored in the presence of all your fellow guests. For everyone who exalts himself will be humbled, and he who humbles himself will be exalted."

It was a star-studded affair. Jesus had attracted the attention of the prominent religious leaders. This particular Pharisee, in turn, had attracted Jesus into his home. He was throwing a banquet. This was no mere "come-on-over-for-some-burgers." Banquets in those days were social events that established the pecking order for the community. Here reputations were won and greatness was vied for.

Now just because Jesus was the honored guest does not mean that he was especially well-liked. In fact, this is the third time in Luke that Jesus attends a meal in a Pharisees' home. The first ended in a fight when Jesus allowed a woman with a reputation to wash his feet (Luke 7:36ff). The second ended in a fight when Jesus neglected to wash his hands (Luke 11:37ff). This one doesn't end so well, either.

You just know trouble's brewing when you read the words, "One Sabbath." This is the literary equivalent to the pounding chords in the movie "Jaws." You just know somebody's about to get bit! It gets worse. Jesus is in the same room with a sick man. When you have disease, Jesus, and the Sabbath at the same place and at the same time, it is a lightning rod for controversy. You expect the Pharisees to explode any second. Undoubtedly they did. But that is not what Luke wants to talk about. Rather, he records Jesus' diatribe against his host. Lest you think that a bit rude, we must remember, the Pharisee started it. He is the one who invited Jesus over with ulterior motives. He is the one who "carefully watched" Jesus (v. 1; cf. 6:7; 20:20). And he is the one who, in all likelihood, planted the ill man to see if Jesus would take the bait. Boy, did he! Now he is on a roll.

First he addresses the issue of Sabbath healing. The words are familiar. "How dare you care for an ox on the Sabbath and ignore a child of Abraham!" We've heard that tune before. Jesus moves to the second stanza: Seating arrangements. All around the room were fancy cushions for the guests to enjoy. There was, however, a specific hierarchy of seats. The more prominent you were, the closer to the host you would be seated. In a society where honor is a more valuable currency than money, this type of recognition was pretty important. In fact, in those days people would give away great sums of money to gain honor. (We seem to do the opposite.) Jesus is not just spanking them for being selfish lads. He is accosting one of their most cherished cultural values — honor and shame.

He argues against self-seeking. He is not merely saying "don't be selfish" or "wait your turn." He is saying, "Deliberately humble yourself and let God look after your honor." This idea is captured in verse 11, "For everyone who exalts himself will be humbled, and he who humbles himself will be exalted." This theology of humility permeates Jesus' preaching. It is one of the core values of Jesus and an essential foundation of following him.

Again, Jesus is not assaulting pride *per se.* He is assaulting our most cherished slogan, "Look out for #1." It is not thinking too highly of oneself that is the problem. It is thinking about one's self, period! Indeed, there is a childishness in seeking chief seats that is reminiscent of two boys fighting for the front seat. For this reason, such self-seeking is offensive and stupid. It is more than this, however. It is downright dangerous. It blossoms into a viciousness that is socially devastating. Watch:

This vignette begins and ends in essentially the same way. It opens with a sick man whose needs are not met because of prominent men's warped priorities. It ends with Jesus rebuking his host for inviting the wealthy instead of the poor. Again, poor people are ignored while the rich get fat. Both are a result of a single mind: Look out for #1. It is not merely the worldly and cowardly who selfishly cater to their pride. It is also the extremely religious. We are not so distant from the Pharisees. Whether it's cushions or kudos, we can be savagely relentless in pursuing recognition, even for banquets that honor Jesus. This is a most difficult text. For it calls us to abandon the contest for self-aggrandizement, and replace it with service for the least and the lost. "Who then will be jealous for my honor?" you ask. Jesus answers, "God." "What if he forgets? What if no one else notices? What if I don't get what I deserve?" At these questions Jesus simply shakes his head, turns softly on his heels and walks away.

Further Reading: Luke 14:1-24.

Ponderable Questions: Can you think of a time that you refused to promote yourself but that God saw to it that you were recognized? How did you feel after that? What would change in your life if you truly had an "audience of One"? How could you implement these ideas this week?

Considerations for Prayer: "Lord, help me care about your opinion alone."

How to Make Heaven Dance

{Luke 15:1-8,11-13; § 116}

Now the tax collectors and "sinners" were all gathering around to hear him. But the Pharisees and the teachers of the law muttered, "This man welcomes sinners and eats with them." Then Jesus told them this parable: "Suppose one of you has a hundred sheep and loses one of them. Does he not leave the ninety-nine in the open country and go after the lost sheep until he finds it? And when he finds it, he joyfully puts it on his shoulders and goes home. Then he calls his friends and neighbors together and says, 'Rejoice with me; I have found my lost sheep.' I tell you that in the same way there will be more rejoicing in heaven over one sinner who repents than over ninety-nine righteous persons who do not need to repent. Or suppose a woman has ten silver coins and loses one. Does she not light a lamp, sweep the house and search carefully until she finds it? . . . Jesus continued: "There was a man who had two sons. The younger one said to his father, 'Father, give me my share of the estate.' So he divided his property between them. "Not long after that, the younger son got together all he had, set off for a distant country and there squandered his wealth in wild living. . . .

This trilogy of parables is perhaps the best known in all the Gospels. What is less well-known is the argument that prompted it. Jesus was hanging around with a bunch of scalawags. There were tax-collectors, prostitutes, bookies, junkies, and folks from MTV. The theological term for such people is "icky." Let's not imagine that this was a minor violation. Jesus is not just acting as a bleeding heart. His behavior is threatening the very ethical system of Judaism. Their teachers hammered away at holiness. Their people were to be set apart from other nations. They acted, dressed, and ate differently. If you take away their difference, then what was left to separate them from all the riffraff that was headed for hell? Jesus, on the other hand, introduced a morality of compassion. That is, the sick need a physician, not the healthy; sinners need repentance which is most often prompted by love. Notice, these two ethical systems are diametrically opposed. The Pharisees teach people to get in the center of the box; Jesus orders them outside the box. No wonder this was such a hot topic!

The point of all three parables is God's unmitigated joy at the repentance of a lost sinner. The first story targets men in the field; the second, women in their homes. Both stories, so true to life, capture the imagination of Jesus' listeners. Both stories are the very kinds of things that happen weekly in every Palestinian village. No so with the third parable. Here Jesus introduces several details that are so outrageous that they would never happen outside God's upside-down kingdom.

First, by asking for his inheritance early, the younger son is practically telling his father to drop dead. Perhaps such requests were made on *rare* occasions, but it is highly unlikely. What is really outrageous is that the father granted his request. You can almost hear the huff of Jesus' audience as they say under their breath, "Oh come on! That would never happen."

Second, this Jewish boy descends into a pigsty. That's a long way down from a noble farming family. Here he comes to his senses and decides to return to his father. In fact, like many of us in such straits, he memorizes a speech (vv. 18-19). He knows exactly what he is going to say. When he arrives home, however, he only gets half of it out before his father cuts him off (vv. 21-22). In his excitement, the father begins to bark out orders to the servants. He calls for a new garment, a signet ring, and sandals. No boy of his was going to walk around like a slave. All of this is pretty unlikely. The boy had shamed the family and reduced their resources in the community. It is not likely that he would be welcomed so freely back into the family. You can almost hear the whispered tones among Jesus' listeners. On the one side of the room the sinners were saying, "He's talking about us. I like this story!" On the other side they were scandalized, "That's not fair; it's not reasonable!" And it wasn't.

Third, when the father saw the son from a long way off, he girded up his loins (which must have been quite a sight) and ran to his son. You must understand, in the Middle East, men don't run. It is seen as degrading. Only a slave or a crook would need to run. The slower you can afford to move, the more dignity you obviously have. The father, overcome by great love, became vulnerable to his son. He threw propriety and dignity out the window and became as giddy as a schoolboy. You can hear them say, "If the father represents God, you are saying God demeaned himself because of a stupid, rebellious child." That is exactly what happened. In fact, the only time God ever ran was when you returned home, and he ran toward you.

I remember telling this story to Linda. She is a single black mother in a small town of eastern Kansas. I was preaching a revival there, and the preacher had taken me over to her house to share the gospel. He took her son into an adjacent room so we could talk without interruption. As I shared with her how God loves her, the words deflected off her past and fell lifelessly to the floor. So I reminded her of this story. She didn't remember it. So I summarized it: "You know, the one about the farmer with two sons." "I've never heard that story before," she said. "Oh sure you have," I replied. "The younger one took half the inheritance into a distance country and squandered it." She looked at me with a blank stare and said, "I've never heard that story." I couldn't believe my ears. If you've never shared this story with someone else for the very first time, you really need to — it's a hoot!

We started at the beginning, not missing a single detail. When I got to the part of the pigsty, she suddenly realized that I was no longer talking about a Palestinian farmer boy, but a single black mother in Kansas. When the son decided to return home and his father saw him from a long way off, I asked her, "Linda, do you know what happened next?" She leaned forward on the edge of her tattered sofa and said, "No, what happened . . . What happened?!" It had now become autobiographical for her. Slowly, deliberately, I finished the story, "When the father saw the son at a distance, he ran to him with open arms and embraced him. He threw him a party and welcomed him home." Her eyes welled up with tears and she choked out just one word: "Really?!" My eyes followed suit and I choked out just one word: "Really!!"

Further Reading: Luke 15:1-32.

Ponderable Questions: Honestly, are you closer to the Pharisees of this story or to the sinners? Why is it that we so quickly forget the stench of the pigsty? Why do you think God gets so giddy about people repenting? List some practical ways in which we can add to the celebration.

Considerations for Prayer: Pray for laborers for the fields that are white (Matt. 9:37-38).

Lazarus Raised from the Dead

56

{John 11:17-27; § 118}

On his arrival, Jesus found that Lazarus had already been in the tomb for four days. Bethany was less than two miles from Jerusalem, and many Jews had come to Martha and Mary to comfort them in the loss of their brother. When Martha heard that Jesus was coming, she went out to meet him, but Mary stayed at home. "Lord," Martha said to Jesus, "if you had been here, my brother would not have died. But I know that even now God will give you whatever you ask." Jesus said to her, "Your brother will rise again." Martha answered, "I know he will rise again in the resurrection at the last day." Jesus said to her, "I am the resurrection and the life. He who believes in me will live, even though he dies; and whoever lives and believes in me will never die. Do you believe this?" "Yes, Lord," she told him, "I believe that you are the Christ, the Son of God, who was to come into the world."

Jesus escaped from Jerusalem after an assassination attempt at the last festival. It was December, likely in A.D. 32. He now finds himself in the backwaters of Perea, a healthy distance from the religious leaders of Jerusalem. Suddenly a fleet-footed messenger arrives with some bad news: Lazarus is dying. This presents a problem. Lazarus lives in Bethany, just two miles east of Jerusalem. For Jesus to return to Judea now would be dangerous. Thomas is well aware of this fact and even offers to accompany Jesus there and to die with him (v. 16).

Rather than running off to "save the day," Jesus sits tight for another 48 hours. By that time Lazarus is dead. Add two more days for travel, and decomposition has set in. Lazarus has been entombed for four days when Jesus arrives. This places Jesus at the grave a full day after Jewish superstition said that the departed spirit finally left the corpse and headed for its eternal abode. There is no question in anyone's mind: Lazarus was truly dead. He is past the point of no return.

I suppose any time someone is raised from the dead, it could be described as extraordinary. But Lazarus' resuscitation is particularly striking. It was the last of the seven signs in John and provided the platform for Jesus' own resurrection. Furthermore, it contains the fifth and final "I AM" statement in John, "I am the resurrection and the life. He who believes in me will live and not die." This story is the pinnacle of the book, and it contains the key elements of Jesus' purpose: He brings the dead to life through faith in him. He doesn't merely offer life. He offers himself, and his very presence infuses life into our existence.

When Mary hears that Jesus has arrived, she races to meet him. Her sadness erupts in these words, "Lord, if only you had been here, my brother would not have died." She still confesses faith in him, but it is a bit watery. She still has some obscure hope that Jesus can ultimately, someday, eschatologically, make it right. Yet there he stands, ready to do more than she can hope for. Jesus is saddened, not because Martha's faith is misplaced, but because it is too small. Jesus doesn't merely want faith that looks to a better future. He craves for us to consume him in such a real way that he envelops the very real rough-and-tumble existence we face today.

Martha talks theology with Jesus. Mary, on the other hand, has a very different encounter with Jesus. When she arrives, she confronts Jesus with the very same sentence as did Martha. Those words must have been the choral refrain of their home for the last week, "If only Jesus had been here." While the words are the same, these two sisters are quite different. Their identical declaration elicited a wildly different response from the Master. On the lips of Martha, they evoke a theological discussion. Coming from Mary, they rouse deep emotions. When Mary says, "Lord, if you had only been here," Jesus is moved to agitation, not at Mary but at death itself which shrouded this woman he so cherished. In fact, the word translated "deeply moved" (*embrimaomai*, v. 33) is normally rendered "anger." It is the word used to describe the snorting of a disgruntled horse.

Jesus is disturbed at the whole situation. He hates what he sees here. It is not so much the women's lack of faith as it is the shroud that death places over those he loves. He wants his friends to believe in him but they can't see through the darkness of death, the light of life that stands before them. It is time to lift the veil. Now here is something strange. Jesus knows what he is about to do. He has been planning it for four days. There at the gateway of the grave he is ready to perform his most extraordinary miracle to date. One would expect Jesus to say, "All right everybody, just watch this!" He doesn't. Rather, he looks around and is captured by the moment. There are friends and family looking for hope in vain. In their eyes is only deep sadness. As Jesus turns to look at Mary, her own grief overwhelms him. There it sits in verse 35: "Jesus wept." The shortest verse in the Bible captures the entire heart of God. Although Jesus knows what is about to transpire, he cannot help but be moved by Mary's sorrow. He is still sovereign over the situation, yet somehow vulnerable to our own suffering. Yes, I think that's it. Our sovereign Lord became vulnerable to us because of his own immense love. Perhaps he still weeps.

Further Reading: John 11:1-44.

Ponderable Questions: Jesus knew what he was about to do; why did he still weep outside the tomb? Is it possible that Jesus is vulnerable to our suffering? Why might Jesus weep over your life right now? How does that make you feel? Do you think your life elicits the "Mary" or the "Martha" response from Jesus?

Considerations for Prayer: Read Romans 8:26. Don't say a word. Simply allow the Holy Spirit to groan for you.

Ten Leaping Lepers

{Luke 17:12-19; § 120a}

As he was going into a village, ten men who had leprosy met him. They stood at a distance and called out in a loud voice, "Jesus, Master, have pity on us!" When he saw them, he said, "Go, show yourselves to the priests." And as they went, they were cleansed. One of them, when he saw he was healed, came back, praising God in a loud voice. He threw himself at Jesus' feet and thanked him—and he was a Samaritan. Jesus asked, "Were not all ten cleansed? Where are the other nine? Was no one found to return and give praise to God except this foreigner?" Then he said to him, "Rise and go; your faith has made you well."

After Jesus raised Lazarus, the Sanhedrin wanted them both dead. Why? Well, political tensions are running high between the Jews and the Romans. Jesus' escapades are drawing quite a following, which only escalates the problem. It looks like he is gathering guerrillas for a rebel attack. In a nutshell, Jesus isn't safe outside a casket. Because they put an APB out for his arrest, Jesus flees north to the back roads between Samaria and Galilee.

He was in the middle of nowhere when a group of banished lepers called for help. Now, this is the sort of thing Jesus has done before (Matt. 8:1-4). So it comes as no surprise that these guys think he could help. What makes it unique, however, is that nine of them were Jewish and one was a Samaritan. Under no other circumstances is it conceivable that these two ethnic groups would cohabit. Only in such distress would they console such a pariah. When their curse is lifted, their affiliation fails.

This sort of event was foreshadowed by Naaman of old (2 Kgs. 5:8-19). In fact, when Jesus alluded to it in his hometown synagogue, they got so mad they tried to push him off a cliff (Luke 4:16-29). The guy with the black hat winds up being the hero of the story. All the rest were too busy fulfilling the law to return and give thanks to Jesus. It would be easy here to extol the virtues of thankfulness. As important as that may be, it is not the point of this story. Luke, who alone tells this tale, is showing how Jesus' prediction in Nazareth is becoming reality. Those who were formerly deemed dirty turn out to be the ones with the greatest faith. It is Luke alone who relates the synagogue sermon, he alone tells of the "Good" Samaritan (Luke 10:25-37). He will go on to tell of the great reception the Gospel received in Samaria (Acts 8:4-25).

If it were left to Luke alone, one might suspect his own prejudice coming into play. But John also gives us glimpses of faithful Samaritans. The woman of John 4 introduces her whole village to the Master. By sunset they say, "He is the savior of the world." So we might be tempted to garner another lesson from this tale: Those who look like outcasts may be most interested in Jesus. This is often true. People with body piercings and live-in lovers, raucous music and rough language are often most aware of their need for a savior and surprisingly open to Jesus. As important as this message may be, however, it is not the driving force of this text.

Jesus ends by saying, "Rise and go; your faith has made you well." Jesus only said this to three other people: the woman with a flow of blood (Mark 5:34; Luke 8:48); the blind man (Mark 10:52); and the sinful woman who anointed Jesus' feet (Luke 7:50). Now there is a motley crew in desperate straits. Nevertheless, Jesus grants all of them the desire of their heart. In their own way, each demonstrated great faith. Regardless of their status, Jesus honored them. Because when it comes right down to it, the only thing that impresses Jesus is faith. Our gender and job, our health and wealth, and our ethnicity and IQ are all irrelevant to the Lord. The only thing he really asks of us is that we trust him.

Further Reading: 2 Kings 5:8-19.

Ponderable Questions: Who would be considered the "lepers" today? Does it seem true that those who are more radically saved are more thankful to Jesus? What are some of the practical problems with "outsiders" entering the church? How can these problems be addressed?

Considerations for Prayer: Thank God for cleansing "outsiders" in your church. The next time you see them, offer them a word of encouragement.

Is It Lawful to Divorce for Any Reason?

58

{Matthew 19:3-9; § 122}

Some Pharisees came to him to test him. They asked, "Is it lawful for a man to divorce his wife for any and every reason?" "Haven't you read," he replied, "that at the beginning the Creator 'made them male and female,' and said, 'For this reason a man will leave his father and mother and be united to his wife, and the two will become one flesh'? So they are no longer two, but one. Therefore what God has joined together, let man not separate." "Why then," they asked, "did Moses command that a man give his wife a certificate of divorce and send her away?" Jesus replied, "Moses permitted you to divorce your wives because your hearts were hard. But it was not this way from the beginning. I tell you that anyone who divorces his wife, except for marital unfaithfulness, and marries another woman commits adultery."

Normally you wouldn't seek advice about marriage from a single man, but Jesus seems to know a little bit about the subject. Besides, the

Pharisees don't really want advice. What they want is an excuse to lambaste Jesus. So they bring to him this sticky wicket of divorce. It was as much a hot button then as it is today. In fact, there were two raging schools of thought on the subject. The great rabbis that preceded Jesus were Hillel and Shammai. Hillel was the more liberal of the two (that is, if a Pharisee can be called a liberal!). He said a man could divorce his wife for any negligent behavior. This might include insulting her in-laws in public, burning his supper, even growing old and ugly. Shammai, on the other hand, taught that only outright adultery was adequate grounds for divorce. Both arguments are based on Deuteronomy 24:1-4. They are trying to put Jesus in the cross fire of their ecclesiastical skirmish. As usual, he rises above it.

Rather than basing his theology of marriage on Deuteronomy 24, he goes all the way back to Genesis 2. "God's intention for marriage," he says, "is lifelong fidelity." Jesus argues that marriage stands on the two pillars of "leaving" and "cleaving." In other words, what makes a marriage work is when a man and woman make each other their primary commitment, even above their nuclear families. This includes, of course, sexual fidelity. If either of these two pillars (primary commitment and sexual fidelity) are violated, the marriage crumbles.

In the simplest terms, when a partner violates sexual fidelity, it is called "adultery." When one violates primary commitment, it is called "divorce." The Pharisees, who mostly follow Hillel's rules, willy-nilly divorce their wives. They accost Jesus with the question, "Don't you think that's okay?" "NO!" Jesus says, "Divorce is NOT okay." Moses only commanded a certificate of divorce to protect women, not to grant men permission. Then he dropped the bombshell: divorce is just like adultery. We've been stumbling over those words ever since! Jesus is certainly not saying that divorce is equivalent to adultery, that is, that they are one and the same act. There is a big difference between the two. He is not saying divorce and adultery are the same but that their consequences are identical. In other words, a woman who is divorced suffers the same ravages as an adulteress. She is thrown back into a predatorial male world, she suffers loss of income and security, she is looked upon with suspicion, and she is lonely and perhaps a single mother. Is the divorcee an adulteress? NO! But she does find herself in the same boat.

What does this say about remarriages? At least this: no second marriage is best. God's design is for a man and a woman to stay married for life. Every second marriage imports some degree of infidelity and suffering. This is not to say that a second marriage cannot be healthy, happy, and God-honoring. But it can never be God's best plan. Are remarried couples living in perpetual adultery? No! Of course not! Jesus is not saying that divorce is adultery, but its consequences are the same. Likewise, remarriage is not the act of adultery, but it contributes to the ultimate dissolution of the first marriage and thus brings about the same consequences of adultery. That is, remarriage puts a nail in the coffin of the first marriage. Should we then remain single? Not necessarily. Sometimes remarriage is the best of two inferior options. Once we sin, we often have no good options left. It is kind of like taking a gulp of tea that is way too hot — whatever you do next is wrong. Remarriage may be your best option, but it always has some negative connotations. That does not mean you live in perpetual sin, but that we all perpetually live in a fallen world.

This whole discussion has caused quite a stir. Yet there is something more important going on in the text. Here a group of Pharisees come to Jesus. Likely, many of them had been divorced. They ask him this question in order to trip him up. Instead, he turns the tables and exposes their hearts. These guys would never commit adultery. That would be sinful. Yet they will divorce their wives when the consequences are identical! Such is the nature of religious banter. Our theologizing over legalistic intricacies allows us to judge others and justify ourselves. Meanwhile, our actions are mean and destructive. The contemporary debate over divorce typically misses the mark as widely as the Pharisees did. We sit in church and rail about rising divorce rates while our single contingent wails for love and pleads for compassion. Our preaching oozes with ostentatious platitudes about moral purity while lonely hearts bleed. We could do with fewer edicts if we had more compassion, with less law if we had more love, and with loosened standards if we had a firmer embrace.

Further Reading: Deuteronomy 24:1-4.

Ponderable Questions: What is God's plan for marriage? What is God's plan for divorced people? How can we show compassion for divorcees in practical and responsible ways? In what ways does God feel the pain of divorce in the spiritual unfaithfulness of his people?

Considerations for Prayer: Meditate on how God could feel the pain of divorce through our unfaithfulness to him (Jas. 4:4).

Rich Men in the Kingdom

{Matthew 19:16-23; § 124}

Now a man came up to Jesus and asked, "Teacher, what good thing must I do to get eternal life?" "Why do you ask me about what is good?" Jesus replied. "There is only One who is good. If you want to enter life, obey the commandments." "Which ones?" the man inquired. Jesus replied, "'Do not murder, do not commit adultery, do not steal, do not give false testimony, honor your father and mother,' and 'love your neighbor as yourself.'" "All these I have kept," the young man said. "What do I still lack?" Jesus answered, "If you want to be perfect, go, sell your possessions and give to the poor, and you will have treasure in heaven. Then come, follow me." When the young man heard this, he went away sad, because he had great wealth. Then Jesus said to his disciples, "I tell you the truth, it is hard for a rich man to enter the kingdom of heaven. Again I tell you, it is easier for a camel to go through the eye of a needle than for a rich man to enter the kingdom of God."

This guy would make the perfect convert. He is young — he would improve the demographics of the group. He is a well-respected community leader — he would make a perfect board member. He is morally impeccable and has been raised in a religious family. He is rich and he tithes. This is exactly the kind of person preachers drool over. Jesus sends him away sad and empty-handed. It looks like the Master needs a lesson in church growth. He's not being very seeker sensitive!

This respectful young man kneels before Jesus and asks a very good question. No, actually, he asked the very best question: "What must I do to be saved?" He asks about good deeds which are essential to salvation. Jesus replies, "Only God is good, and he laid out his moral expectations in the Ten Commandments. Follow them and you'll be okay." The problem is this: the young man has been following these decrees since he was a little boy, and he still senses a critical gap. He longs for God but is still estranged. How can he bridge the gap?

From this side of the cross it's pretty easy to answer his question. Jesus is the only way to the Father (John 14:6). He alone can bridge the gap and bring salvation (Acts 4:12). If this young man is to fellowship with God, he must first follow Jesus. That will be difficult because he has a ball and chain about his ankle. His fortune is his hindrance. It's not that his wealth is wicked, just distracting. If he doesn't shed the shackles, he has no hope of chasing after Jesus.

This idea of money being a barricade to God is a new concept to the young man. You see, in the Old Testament, wealth was one of the indications of God's blessing. Most of the money talk up to Malachi is positive. The righteous are rewarded. Once we get to Matthew, however, the tables have turned. Money becomes a terribly seductive detriment to one's quest for God. It teaches us to trust in ourselves rather than in the Divine (Rev. 3:14-22). It is the foundation of favoritism in the church (Jas. 2:1-8). It engulfs us in worry for this world (Matt. 6:25-34). Materialism is so dangerous, in fact, that Jesus says you have to choose between it and him (Matt. 6:24), for no one can serve two masters.

We still try, however. We imagine that we can pursue Jesus and seek money at the same time. In fact, we print this strange sentence on our coinage: "In God we trust." This will always be a true statement. The question is, "Which god?" We have not believed Jesus when he said that it is easier for a camel to get through the eye of a needle than a rich man to enter heaven. Jesus' call here is not to ascetic poverty but to single-minded focus. Therefore, having money is not the problem. It is allowing money to control us that is the problem. Theoretically, a person could control large amounts of money and still be driven only by Jesus. However, most of us vastly overestimate our ability to tame the beast of materialism.

The solution is not likely a massive garage sale (although most homes would benefit from the surgery of simplification). It is not that selling our property is too radical. Rather, it will likely prove too shallow a surgery. We don't need an amputation but a bone-marrow transplant. We have been weaned on Western materialism. We've bought into the rampant accumulation of wealth. If Jesus is to be our single source of sustenance, we must think very differently than we do now.

It would be easier if there was a single act or set standard for materialism. If we could just say a house of 80k or a car of 10k is the upper limit and leave it at that. Black and white rules and quick fixes, however, are obviously unsatisfactory. This battle will be long and arduous. We will likely fight perpetually against the onslaught of materialism to the end of our existence in this society. Our lack of precision, however, should not translate into lack of action. This passage calls for vigilance in incisively examining our prioritization of Jesus. It behooves believers to constantly increase their sacrificial giving to the Kingdom both in time and material resources. We must relentlessly push the boundaries of our budgets to attack excess and the false security of wealth in order to rapaciously and tenaciously grasp simplicity. As the wealthiest nation in the history of the world, it is nearly inevitable that we will underestimate how closely we resemble a camel.

Further Reading: Matthew 6:24-34; 19:24-30; Luke 16:1-31; James 2:1-8.

Ponderable Questions: What do these texts teach us about materialism in the life of a disciple? Is it really all that dangerous? Our culture and situation are quite different than the disciples'. Have the rules changed for us with money? Why is it so hard for us to realistically listen to Jesus' talk about money?

Considerations for Prayer: Ask for ears to hear.

Right and Left, and Up and Down

{Mark 10:35-37,41-45; § 125b}

Then James and John, the sons of Zebedee, came to him. "Teacher," they said, "we want you to do for us whatever we ask." "What do you want me to do for you?" he asked. They replied, "Let one of us sit at your right and the other at your left in your glory." . . . When the ten heard about this, they became indignant with James and John. Jesus called them together and said, "You know that those who are regarded as rulers of the Gentiles lord it over them, and their high officials exercise authority over them. Not so with you. Instead, whoever wants to become great among you must be your servant, and whoever wants to be first must be slave of all. For even the Son of Man did not come to be served, but to serve, and to give his life as a ransom for many."

How bodacious would you have to be to walk up to Jesus, right in front of your colleagues, and ask for special privileges?! Granted, James and John have a 66% majority vote in the inner council of three.

Nonetheless, this is still a bit presumptuous. It is actually even worse than it at first appears. For Jesus has just predicted his own sacrificial death. So the conversation goes something like this. Jesus: "Fellas, I'm going to lay down my life." James and John: "Can we be your #1 and #2 in the kingdom?"

It really is outrageous, but not so different than today. Before we walk or talk, we learn that the louder we are, the more attention and trinkets we get. We cry for food, pout for toys, and in the really tough cases we revert to tantrums. As toddlers we perfect the art of egocentrism. Posing for cameras and being first in line were practiced disciplines. Our parents prompted us to assert ourselves. They fostered in us a competitive spirit that was already latent and huge. In school our teachers and coaches goaded us to be the best and brightest. We heard it from the sidelines a thousand times: "Get aggressive out there!" The cheerleaders of our lives all seemed to agree — if you beat the other guy to the punch, you can be the best. After all, that is what life is really all about.

In the din of selfish ambition and egocentric aggression, it is nearly impossible to hear the call of Jesus to self-denial. Even though the theology of humility is inextricably woven through the pages of the New Testament, it is as difficult for us to catch as it was for the Twelve. The idea of a basin and a towel (John 13:1-7) or "the first shall be last" (1 Cor. 9:19; 1 Pet. 5:2-6) or childlikeness (Mark 10:13-16) often seems beyond our ability to comprehend. Jesus has already talked about it plenty. Now it is time for him to illustrate it in a way that none can miss. In verse 45 Jesus lays out his program for ministry: "The Son of Man did not come to be served, but to serve, and to give his life as a ransom for many." This is the way of the cross. By laying down his life, Jesus rescued us from death. He himself is the ransom, the payment for us. He who shared the glory of God became the servant of all. The cross is not merely an event for Jesus, it was a way of life that he calls all his followers to adopt.

Jesus tried to get James and John to understand this with the metaphors of "cup" and "baptism." Both illustrations speak of suffering. They ask for exalted positions, and Jesus only promises persecution. He is not saying, "No, you can't be exalted." Rather, he is saying, "The way to exaltation in this upside-down kingdom is through suffering." Then Jesus showed all of us the way through his own passion.

God's kingdom is a very strange place. Everything is backward here. The king is a slave that died for the ransom of others. The greatest are servants; the humble exalted. The mighty are obliterated; the lost are found. The blind see, and those who see are blinded. The rich are poor, but those who sell everything find a treasure of enormous proportions. To live one must die, and when we forsake our families we are adopted and rewarded with 10,000% interest.

Let's be clear about one thing. We're not talking about being rewarded in heaven for suffering on earth. We're arguing that the *modus operandi* of the kingdom of God is the way of the cross. We are called to self-denial as a means to exaltation. It is the mystery of the Beatitudes. It is the imitation of Christ. It is embedded in our baptism and laced through the Lord's Supper. It is the grand theme of Christianity. Yet it is a more difficult concept than the Trinity, the sovereignty of God, and predestination all wrapped into one. If we don't get it, we cannot be Jesus' disciples.

Further Reading: Matthew 20:20-28; 1 Corinthians 9:19; 1 Peter 5:2-6; "Theology of Humility" — available in electronic form from College Press.

Ponderable Questions: How were we taught growing up to promote ourselves? How is this related to the sins we struggle with? Explain how the cross is the premier example of self-abnegation. In what ways do you need to implement this text in your own walk with Jesus?

Considerations for Prayer: Meditate on the cross of Christ and how to incorporate it as a way of life.

Bold, Blind Bartimaeus

{Mark 10:46-52; § 126}

Then they came to Jericho. As Jesus and his disciples, together with a large crowd, were leaving the city, a blind man, Bartimaeus (that is, the Son of Timaeus), was sitting by the roadside begging. When he heard that it was

> Jesus of Nazareth, he began to shout, "Jesus, Son of David, have mercy on me!" Many rebuked him and told him to be quiet, but he shouted all the more, "Son of David, have mercy on me!" Jesus stopped and said, "Call him." So they called to the blind man, "Cheer up! On your feet! He's calling you." Throwing his cloak aside, he jumped to his feet and came to Jesus. "What do you want me to do for you?" Jesus asked him. The blind man said, "Rabbi, I want to see." "Go," said Jesus, "your faith has healed you." Immediately he received his sight and followed Jesus along the road.

Blindness is a persistent problem in third-world countries. Often children are born blind because of unsanitary conditions at birth. It is really very sad. Most of these unfortunates are reduced to meandering through overcrowded streets, begging for a few shekels. They are generally treated like parking meters. They are a mild nuisance on every street corner, easily pacified with the excess coins in your pocket. As long as they keep their distance and sit quietly, we'll put up with them. On this particular day, Bartimaeus refused to do either.

It is now a week before Jesus' final ascent to Jerusalem, where he will meet his demise. He has attracted a good bit of attention in Perea from his preaching and healing in the last couple of months. His considerable entourage makes its way toward the Holy City as Passover nears. Crowds from all over the Middle East are beginning to funnel through this desert oasis about the same time as Jesus. The population swells as does the excitement about this potential Messiah. The people of Jericho hear that Jesus & Co. are coming. They line the streets, waiting to catch a glimpse of this esoteric prophet and perhaps even to see another extraordinary miracle. On this particular day, they'll not be disappointed.

As Jesus approaches the city, the crowd behind him swells. With every step he takes, those who line the streets fall in behind. There must have been a good bit of jostling for position, lots of shoving and shouting, and hundreds of crooked necks. Above the din comes a cry, "Son of David, have mercy on me." It was loud and persistent. The locals recognize it is Bartimaeus. What an embarrassment! This is not the kind of PR that will be good for the reputation of Jericho. They move in swiftly to shut him up in the same way contemporary city officials try to hide the homeless during festivals. But Bartimaeus will not be thwarted. He realizes just how precious and rare is an encounter with Christ. He was right, too. Had he not latched on to Jesus this day, he would never have seen a day in his life.

The more they tried to quiet him, the louder he got. The hubbub reached Jesus and stopped him dead in his tracks. He called for Bartimaeus to come. These "library monitors" who tried to hush him suddenly become his escorts. "Jesus is calling you," they say. He got so excited that he jumped up, leaving his cloak (and probably the panhandled change lying in its folds). The Master asked him what he wanted, which seems pretty self-evident. "I want to see." Permission granted — let the games begin.

You can just sense the jubilation of the parade that must have followed. Shouts of praise shot intuitively to the heavens. Spectators point and ask their neighbor, "Did you see that?" As if anyone could have missed it! Laughter, dance, and jubilation are all natural outbursts. What a great story. However, it is more than an entertaining tale. Receiving sight has serious spiritual ramifications. From the man born blind in John 9 to Saul on the road to Damascus, receiving sight is synonymous with seeing Jesus. Even here Bartimaeus saw Jesus before his eyes were ever opened. That is, he called him by his kosher Messianic title, "Son of David." Because he saw Jesus, Jesus granted him sight. This is a powerful truth that Matthew actually records twice (cf. 9:27-28). This doublet is clearly something to be taken seriously. Bartimaeus and his blind cohorts stand as reminders of our own encounter with Christ. When we come to see Jesus for who he really is, our eyes are opened to the world around us. We see with clarity what was formerly only shadow and blur. Jesus becomes the lens through which life is seen in all its beauty. We see people, politics, media, even ourselves differently. Indeed, each of us can sing with Bartimaeus, "I once was blind, but now I see."

Further Reading: Isaiah 29:18-23.

Ponderable Questions: What was it that Bartimaeus "saw" in Jesus that made him so persistent? How does Bartimaeus illustrate the idea that the rejects are often the most fit for the Kingdom of God? What kinds of things do new converts and "outsiders" seem to understand that long-standing churchgoers miss? Why do folks like Bartimaeus attract Jesus' attention and affection?

Considerations for Prayer: Close your eyes. Sit quietly in darkness. When you're ready, call out to Jesus, "Son of David, have mercy on me."

Little Man Out on a Limb

{Luke 19:1-10; § 127a}

Jesus entered Jericho and was passing through. A man was there by the name of Zacchaeus; he was a chief tax collector and was wealthy. He wanted to see who Jesus was, but being a short man he could not, because of the crowd. So he ran ahead and climbed a sycamore-fig tree to see him, since Jesus was coming that way. When Jesus reached the spot, he looked up and said to him, "Zacchaeus, come down immediately. I must stay at your house today." So he came down at once and welcomed him gladly. All the people saw this and began to mutter, "He has gone to be the guest of a 'sinner.'" But Zacchaeus stood up and said to the Lord, "Look, Lord! Here and now I give half of my possessions to the poor, and if I have cheated anybody out of anything, I will pay back four times the amount." Jesus said to him, "Today salvation has come to this house, because this man, too, is a son of Abraham. For the Son of Man came to seek and to save what was lost."

Jubilant is probably too tame a word for this scene. Jesus has already made his presence felt in Jericho by healing Bartimaeus. The party takes to the city streets. Jericho explodes with celebration. Everyone in the city is keenly interested in seeing this wonder-worker. That's quite amazing, actually, since this city was a multicultural melting pot. Here in this desert oasis lay the crossroads of commerce. It was the intersection of Syria and Arabia, Egypt and Mesopotamia. Because of its strategic location, it was a circus of humanity. There were soldiers and pilgrims, thieves and caravans, prostitutes and Orthodox Jews. In the middle of the mix was, of course, the Roman IRS. This group of political pirates took advantage of the economic boom and taxed everything that either moved or stood still.

The Romans sold taxation rights to the highest bidder. Whatever a man could squeeze out of the locals beyond what he promised Rome was his to keep. There are some obvious and inherent flaws in this system. Namely, it fostered greed and extortion. Whoever could master this sinister trade would rise to the top as a very wealthy man. In this town his name was Zacchaeus. He was head and shoulders above the rest — at least economically. When everyone converged on the city streets to see this Messianic hopeful, Zacchaeus's curiosity got the best of him. Along with his clients he just had to see what all the fuss was about.

Problem: Zacchaeus was too short to see anything. Furthermore, after bullying all his clients in the IRS office, they're not about to let him weasel his way to the front-row seats on the street. Short people sometimes have to resort to extraordinary measures to get where they want. He ran up the street and climbed a sycamore-fig tree. He went out on a limb to see Jesus. There he is, in a pin-striped toga, up in a tree, way beneath his dignity. He just *had* to see Jesus. What he didn't count on was Jesus' seeing him.

When Jesus stopped and called Zacchaeus out of the tree, the crowd was scandalized! (With the possible exception of Matthew, of course.) Of all the dirty, rotten scumbags, Jesus chose the worst. There were hundreds of people who would have gladly hosted Jesus in their homes — good homes, with kosher food, and children on the honor role. Zacchaeus didn't deserve to have Jesus come to his house. That's precisely the point.

The story ends with Jesus' purpose statement, "The Son of Man came to seek and to save what was lost." He took a tax collector and proclaimed him a child of Abraham. It is both scandalous and wonderful. It was scandalous because Jesus graced a sinner. It was wonderful because the sinner was transformed and graced the poor of his community.

You know, Jesus' purpose has not changed. He is still in the business of search and rescue. In fact, there are two other purpose statements given by Jesus that really need to be saddled next to this one. The first comes from Mark 10:45 (and Matt. 20:28): The Son of Man came not to be served but to serve and to give his life as a ransom for many. The second comes from John 10:10, "I have come that they may have life and have it to the full." Laid side by side, these mission statements bring Jesus' life into focus. He came for the down-and-outers, like lepers and bleeding women, as well as for the up-and-outers, like Zacchaeus. He gave his life on the cross so that we might truly live. This amazing grace transforms us and enables us to extend grace to others no more deserving than ourselves. We take his legacy of love and "pay it forward."

Further Reading: Write these three verses on a 3×5 card and post it where you can read it daily for a month: Mark 10:45; Luke 19:10; John 10:10.

Ponderable Questions: Based on this story, fill out the details of the following sermon outline: I. Jesus knows you; II. Jesus loves you; III. Jesus needs you. Find someone this week to share this message with.

Considerations for Prayer: "Lord, help my life mission to be yours."

Encounters with Christ

The Final Week

A Parade Fit for a King

{Mark 11:7-11a; § 128b}

When they brought the colt to Jesus and threw their cloaks over it, he sat on it. Many people spread their cloaks on the road, while others spread branches they had cut in the fields. Those who went ahead and those who followed shouted, "Hosanna! Blessed is he who comes in the name of the Lord! Blessed is the coming kingdom of our father David! Hosanna in the highest!" Jesus entered Jerusalem and went to the temple.

A little donkey ride hardly seems like a big hullabaloo. However, if we see it through an ancient lens, it suddenly looms large. First, we need to realize that riding a donkey into Jerusalem was what kings did at their inauguration (cf. 1 Kgs. 1:33). Furthermore, there's a mess of Messianic prophecies about a coming king that played against this parade (Ezek. 33:1-5; Zech. 9:9; 14:1-5; Ps. 118:26). The fact that this crowd starts to sing about it indicates they were very much in tune with Jesus' intentions. They came from all over to visit the Holy City during the Passover festival. We must understand how spiritually charged they got as they walked up the steep hills to their ancient capital city. We must understand how disgruntled and angry they were about being oppressed by the Romans. We must understand that they were longing for an end to their exile. Granted, they lived in Palestine, but because they were not an independent state, they couldn't fully celebrate God's release from their captivity. For it still hung about them in the form of a Roman albatross.

The news that Jesus was coming spread through Jerusalem like a grass fire. Thousands line the steeps of Mt. Olivet awaiting his arrival. Thousands followed in boisterous celebration. The anticipation broke forth in open celebration when Jesus crested the 2,600′ mountain overlooking a panoramic view of the city. The crowds lifted up shouts of praise: "Hosanna to the Son of David; blessed is he who comes in the name of the Lord." Their praise was peppered with words like "kingdom," "David," "Glory in the highest," and "Peace." If Jesus intended the donkey to point to a kingly inauguration, these folks understood clearly what he said. Not only their words pointed to a regal throne, but so do their actions. They laid their cloaks on the ground and began waving palm branches. This activity is unmistakably political and royal. Herod Agrippa is on his way out; Jesus is on his way in.

A year ago at the feeding of the 5,000 they tried to make Jesus king. He refused. Now they get another chance. Jesus rides down the Mount of Olives and heads straight for the Temple some 300′ below. He heads for the hub of Israel, the Holy Place of God. You can see right into the temple mount from Mount Olivet. That also means that you can see Mount Olivet from the temple mount. This is important. All the religious leaders look up to see their worst nightmare: Jesus, with the support of his people, acting like a king. The reason this was so frightening was because the Romans would notice too. Their main garrison was stationed in the Fortress of Antonia at the northwest corner of the temple. They would interpret this as a fomenting coup which needed to be squelched. Blood will be spilt.

We are tempted to say, "Those people just didn't understand. Jesus didn't come as a rival to Herod or the emperor. He came to rule in our hearts." We suggest that Jesus' Jewish supporters were mistaken to follow him as a political ruler rather than a spiritual one. However, Jews never distinguished between the two. There was no such thing as a Jewish king who was not also a spiritual leader. Furthermore, the book of Acts clearly portrays a church that intersects with society in such a way as to create social and political tension. Twenty times in twenty-eight chapters the people of God were arrested, tried, and beaten, before a variety of political authorities, both Jewish and Roman. There is simply no way to argue that the church is merely spiritual and not also a social force to be reckoned with. The dichotomy, I think, is not between the spiritual and political. Rather, it is a difference in how Jesus' political/social program is carried out. The church is to be a socially identifiable group of people as clearly identifiable as this clamoring crowd on the slopes of Mt. Olivet. We differ not in that our interests are isolated to spiritual things. No, we differ in that our agenda is carried out through love and truth rather than power and violence. Jesus is, indeed, a threat to Herod and the Emperor. In hindsight we can see how much damage he did to their reigns. Jesus and his people conquer through a cross rather than a sword. Make no mistake, however, we do still conquer kingdoms.

Further Reading: Ezekiel 33:1-5; Zechariah 9:9; 14:1-5; Psalm 118:15-28; "Kingdom" — available in electronic form from College Press.

Ponderable Questions: In what sense was Jesus a political figure? How did his politics differ from those of Herod or the Sanhedrin? What are the practical differences between Jesus' establishing a church and a kingdom? Which do you really want to be a part of?

Considerations for Prayer: Acclaim Jesus as king — God's final envoy.

A Cursed Fig and a Cleansed Temple

{Mark 11:12-14,20-21; § 129 & 131}

The next day as they were leaving Bethany, Jesus was hungry. Seeing in the distance a fig tree in leaf, he went to find out if it had any fruit. When he reached it, he found nothing but leaves, because it was not the season for figs. Then he said to the tree, "May no one ever eat fruit from you again." And his disciples heard him say it. . . . In the morning, as they went along, they saw the fig tree withered from the roots. Peter remembered and said to Jesus, "Rabbi, look! The fig tree you cursed has withered!"

It is now Monday morning, the day after the triumphal entry. It was a powerful and exciting experience that must have left the disciples ecstatic and exhausted. They follow Jesus back to Jerusalem from their hideout in Bethany. For some reason, they didn't get breakfast. It's not too hard to guess why — Jesus often missed meals because he was so engrossed in ministry. This is going to be another one of those whirlwind weeks.

It is apparently midmorning, and Jesus is hungry. Since the Jews generally ate their first of two meals around 10 a.m., we might guess it is well-nigh time for brunch. Somewhere along the two-mile trek from Bethany to Jerusalem, Jesus spied a fig tree. Now granted, it was still a bit early for full-grown figs. But the green immature fruit should have been abundant. They're a bit bitter, but still edible, particularly when you're feeling a little "eleven o'clockish."

When Jesus caught up with the tree, he discovered it had faked him out. Its lush green leaves promised the fruit it refused to bear. No buds now mean no figs later. The Master appears to be miffed. He curses the tree, "May no one ever eat fruit from you again!" Indeed, this is a strange thing for Jesus to say. Then again, that's nothing new for him. The apostolic band hardly misses a beat in their journey to Jerusalem.

It is now Tuesday morning. Jesus & Co. walk the same trail as the day before. Peter is the first to notice. The cursed tree was now withered from its roots. Any arborist will tell you that's a pretty immediate demise of a flourishing tree. The stunned disciples stop and stare. Jesus begins to apply the lesson of the fig tree to prayer. According to Jesus, there are two things to learn from this. First, with faith, a believer can move mountains, not just fig trees (vv. 22-23). Second, as Jesus' followers, our prayers are authoritative. They can even call God to forgive other's sins, or if need be, to hold sin against someone (v. 25). This promise is extraordinary, but not unqualified. That is, there are some parameters around this promise of the power of prayer.

This passage is one of Mark's famous sandwiches. He just loves to slip a meaty story in between the slices on either side. The astute will readily recognize that the story of the fig tree pauses between Monday and Tuesday mornings. Between the two, Mark places the account of Jesus' cleansing the temple. When Mark makes a sandwich like this, the "bread" is invariably flavored by the meat. So we must interpret the fig tree in connection with the cleansing. Set side-by-side, it comes out like this: The fig tree is an enacted parable of the unbelieving leaders of Israel. In the same way that Jesus cursed the unproductive tree, so the fruitless temple is doomed to destruction.

Therefore, the two lessons on prayer need to be set in the specific context of unbelieving Israel. The faithless hierarchy looks like a mountain. By faithful prayer it can be tossed into the ocean. When Christians stand in the face of opposition, our prayers and preaching can announce forgiveness as well as punishment. These two lessons on removing mountains and sins are amply illustrated in the book of Acts. The Apostles broke down strongholds, even in the face of fierce and fruitless opposition. Their preaching announced both forgiveness and punishment. Even today, the saga continues. The church of Jesus, through prayer and preaching, demolishes all that stands in the way of the relentless march of the kingdom of God. As God's ambassadors, we still have the authority to announce God's forgiveness as well as his coming judgment. Although the fig tree is dead, its message lives on.

Further Reading: Mark 11:12-25, Matthew 18:19; John 14:13-16; 16:23-26; "Ask" — available in electronic form from College Press.

Ponderable Questions: Are Christians given authority even for imprecatory prayer? If you were to pray "against" something, what would it be? Tell about the last extraordinary prayer that God answered for you? What kind of changes will you make in your prayer life because of this text?

Considerations for Prayer: Ask God to remove some mountain in your life that is contrary to his purposes of winning the lost.

Three Strikes and You're Out!

{Matthew 22:15-46; § 133-136}

Then the Pharisees went out and laid plans to trap him in his words. They sent their disciples to him along with the Herodians. . . . Tell us then, what is your opinion? Is it right to pay taxes to Caesar or not?" . . . Then he said to them, "Give to Caesar what is Caesar's, and to God what is God's." . . . That same day the Sadducees, who say there is no resurrection, came to him with a question. . . . Now then, at the resurrection, whose wife will she be of the seven, since all of them were married to her?" Jesus replied, "You are in error because you do not know the Scriptures or the power of God. . . . He is not the God of the dead but of the living.". . . An expert in the law, tested him with this question: "Teacher, which is the greatest commandment in the Law?" Jesus replied: "'Love the Lord your God with all your heart and with all your soul and with all your mind.' This is the first and greatest commandment. And the second is like it: 'Love your neighbor as yourself.' . . ." While the Pharisees were gathered together, Jesus asked them, "What do you think about the Christ? Whose son is he?"

He marched triumphantly into Jerusalem on Sunday and cleansed the temple on Monday. It is now Tuesday of Jesus' last week, and the Jewish leaders can't allow him to continue unchallenged. He is simply gaining too much momentum. They must stop him here or not at all. Right in the temple courts there will be a deadly duel with rapier wits. Jesus stands on the right with wide-eyed fans behind him. The religious leaders stand on the left. Each of three political wings pushes forward their champion. Let the games begin.

The first to try to trap Jesus were the Herodians. These political allies of Herod had much to lose if Jesus were crowned king. Backed by the Pharisees (odd bedfellows for these political types), they come up with a question sure to snare the Nazarene: "Should we pay taxes to Caesar?" What a great trap! If Jesus says, "Yes," his followers will surely disband in disappointment. After all, what kind of Messiah can't even evade Roman taxation? On the other hand, if he says, "No, don't pay taxes," the Roman troops would eagerly whisk him away as an insurrectionist. Either way, he is out of the way. It was really quite a clever question.

Jesus calls for a coin. Someone in the crowd tosses him a denarius. As he looks at it, the Herodians must have quivered. On the front was a picture of the emperor with this inscription, "Tiberius Caesar, son of the Divine Augustus." Last time I checked, that was blasphemy! What on earth was a good Jew doing with a heretical token in his pocket in the temple? That's what Jesus wants to know. He simply says, "If it has Caesar's picture on it, it must belong to him. Give to Caesar what is Caesar's, give to God what is God's." The implication is clear. They had cowered to Caesar, but not given God his due. The Herodians were amazed at Jesus' response; the crowds were delighted. Strike one.

Next up are the Sadducees. These priestly pontificates controlled the temple mount. They were much more interested in power and pomp than religious matters. Their question about Levitical marriage was designed to make resurrection look ridiculous by comparing it to eternal incest. With this "worst case scenario" they attempt to make Jesus look like an uneducated Fundamentalist, not worthy of serious consideration. Their motives are obvious and blatant. So is Jesus' response, "You're ignorant of both the power of God and his Scriptures!" Then, pulling a text from their cherished Torah, he says, "God is the God of the living not the dead." Jesus' argument is not merely based on the verb tense — "God *is* the God of Abraham, Isaac, and Jacob." Rather, he is suggesting that God is so great that whatever stands in proximity to him will come to life. That is to say, he is a *living* God who causes life to happen! In two short sentences Jesus takes a very old argument and settles accounts. His logic is uncanny, his power uncontested. Even the Pharisees congratulate him on that one! Strike two.

Finally, here come the Pharisees. They are closest to Jesus in theological persuasion and their question is the easiest to answer. He has heard it before from another lawyer in Luke 10:27. "Which is the greatest commandment?" His answer mirrors the one given earlier. "Love God; love people. All other commands are merely subsets of these." The man who asked the question confessed how right the Master was. Strike three.

Jesus scans the competition. It has all been laid waste. With none to ask him any more questions, Jesus has a query of his own. "If the Messiah is David's son, why does he call him Lord?" Psalm 110:1 says, "Yahweh said to my Lord, 'Sit at my right hand until I put your enemies under your feet.'" The argument is complex, but it basically boils down to this: A Jewish father is always greater than his son. How then can David confess the Messiah to be his Lord? They gave no answer. Jesus did. It was because Jesus is not merely David's offspring, but the very son of God. This text, so popular with the Jews, predicts the defeat of all of Jesus' enemies. He is not just quizzing them on the Messiah, he is threatening them. He does that, you know, when one stands in opposition to the Anointed of God.

Jesus encounters his enemies. Their arguments give way to silence as Jesus answers with the power of God. In no uncertain terms he lays waste all opposition. Those who pretend to have Jesus painted in a corner with some philosophic query, will find he has them in a headlock with the very authority of Yahweh. If we do not stand with Jesus, we will soon find ourselves unable to stand at all.

Further Reading: Matthew 22:15-46; Revelation 19:11-21.

Ponderable Questions: Is Jesus always "meek and mild"? Can you think of times he was fierce? How will Jesus look and act when he returns to face his enemies? In light of this, do you think we sometimes treat Jesus too flippantly?

Considerations for Prayer: Acknowledge Jesus as the mighty warrior God.

Seven Deadly Woes

{Matthew 23:1-5a,11-12; § 137}

Then Jesus said to the crowds and to his disciples: "The teachers of the law and the Pharisees sit in Moses' seat. So you must obey them and do everything they tell you. But do not do what they do, for they do not practice what they preach. They tie up heavy loads and put them on men's shoulders, but they themselves are not willing to lift a finger to move them. Everything they do is done for men to see." . . . The greatest among you will be your servant. For whoever exalts himself will be humbled, and whoever humbles himself will be exalted.

Religion can be a nasty business, and the meanest of all men are the protectors of shrines. What makes them so bad is they use the name of God to perpetuate their own power and whitewash their greed with clerical robes. Religious deeds are a convincing disguise even for damnable men. In this chapter, Jesus' critique of the Pharisees reaches its apex for this very reason.

The Master is both sad and angry, and that's a bad combination. He couches his criticism in a series of seven woes. The first six come in pairs, the last one is the *coup de grace*. Before analyzing his critique, a word about "Woe" is in order. This word carries with it several connotations, kind of like when your mother uses your middle name. There is anger, disappointment, sadness, and fury, all rolled into one. The fact that there are seven doesn't bode well for the recipients.

#1 & 2 (vv. 13-15): *Woe to you because you refuse to enter the kingdom of God. In fact, you block the door. Indeed, you travel abroad to make disciples, but you keep them in a narrow cage of legalism.* The Pharisees were highly evangelistic, but about the wrong things. Instead of getting all worked up about the poor and oppressed, they got exercised over Sabbath regulations and legal verbiage.

#3 & 4 (vv. 16-24): *Woe to you because you make silly rules about what vows are valid and which ones you don't have to keep. You even tithe your garden herbs. But you could care less about justice, mercy and faithfulness — the weightier matters of the law.* These guys mastered the persnickety. The important stuff is what they had problems with. They carefully guarded their religious ritual while pummeling hurting people with the very rules they protected.

#5 & 6 (vv. 25-28): *Woe to you because you clean up the outside, but the inside is rotten to the core.* There was nothing in their appearance that was culpable. Just below the surface, however, was putrifaction. They were like bowls that were only washed on the outside. Even worse, they were like whitewashed coffins, full of dead men's bones. Even in English this is not a pretty picture. Exported into Judaism, however, it's far worse.

#7 (vv. 29-36): *Woe to you because you are murderers.* Oh, now that would go over like pork rinds at Passover! The Pharisees vehemently deny any connection with the murder of the ancient prophets. "If we had been alive," they contend, "we would not have participated in their execution!" Jesus disagrees. He suggests that their decoration of the prophets' tombs is actually a celebration of their death. Well, they could deny this all day long. What they won't be able to deny, however, is their own participation in Jesus' execution. In a nutshell Jesus points his finger at them and says, "Like father, like son."

On the surface this text looks like an ancient tirade against an extinct group of religious leaders called the Pharisees. Why, then, would Matthew record it? Why would God preserve it? It's really very simple. Matthew isn't merely pointing a finger at his adversaries, he is holding up a mirror to the church. These Pharisees were the Master's arch rivals. Yet somehow we have imitated them as much as we have our Lord. All too often the self-proclaimed keepers of the kingdom look more like Pharisees than they do Jesus. Not infrequently we share their priorities and flaws.

Let's cut to the chase. The Pharisees are rebuked for three things. The church is often rightly critiqued for the same. First, we can be terribly hypocritical. We make these rules that have little or nothing to do with the Bible. We stack them atop bended backs and proclaim the importance of morality. All the while, behind closed doors, we jump through a series of loopholes. Second, religious leaders can be aggressively self-seeking. They gloat over numbers, wrangle for hegemony, and crave recognition. They are often more interested in what parishioners offer than what they need. Finally, preachers and elders can hide behind the name of God to justify evil behavior. Greed, licentiousness, pride, and power are lightly coated with a veneer of self-righteousness. This text is too critical to leave at A.D. 33. We had better import it to the 21st century and see how well it fits. Jesus is not just talking to "them," he's screaming at "us."

Further Reading: Matthew 23:1-39; "Pharisees" — available in electronic form from College Press.

Ponderable Questions: How have Christians, especially our leaders, often acted like the Pharisees? Are there ways of recognizing Pharisaic behavior in ourselves? What are our motives/reasons for becoming hypocritical? How can we begin to eliminate Phariseeism from our lives?

Considerations for Prayer: Sing, "Create in Me a Clean Heart."

67 A Widow's Mighty Mite 67

{Mark 12:41-44; § 138}

Jesus sat down opposite the place where the offerings were put and watched the crowd putting their money into the temple treasury. Many rich people threw in large amounts. But a poor widow came and put in two very small copper coins, worth only a fraction of a penny. Calling his disciples to him, Jesus said, "I tell you the truth, this poor widow has put more into the treasury than all the others. They all gave out of their wealth; but she, out of her poverty, put in everything — all she had to live on."

Jesus walked out of the temple for what would be the very last time. As he passed the court of the women, he saw off to the side thirteen trumpet-shaped receptacles. These received the various offerings and sacrifices brought by devout worshipers. They were made from brass, so the heavier the coin, the louder the clang. Many rich people took advantage of this fact. They dropped a handful of coins from high above the rim. The clatter captured the crowd's attention. Invariably people crooked their necks to see the latest wealthy benefactor of the temple. Piety and pride thus became the warp and woof of the sacred offerings.

Among these ostentatious worshipers stepped a little old lady. She was a widow down on her luck. She loved God with all her heart, but she was as poor as a church mouse. All she could squeak out was a couple of *mites*. The word itself comes from the root "to peal." Mites were apparently mere shavings of metal, worth 1/64 of a day's wages. They would be almost more of a hassle to count than they were worth. Their "tink" compared to everyone else's "clank" was hardly cause to strike up the band. But Jesus noticed. Not only did he notice, he got so excited that he had to call all the boys and point out how wonderful it was. Considering where they were and when, Jesus' fervor must have raised their expectations. Perhaps they thought Jesus was going to raise the banner of the kingdom right then and there. Maybe he was going to announce his official appointments. Whatever it was, it was going to be big! Imagine their consternation when all the fuss was over a couple of mites!

"Look over there," Jesus said. "Do you see that woman? Guess what she just did. She dropped in two mites into the offering." Perhaps it was Judas who said, "So what's the big deal?" Matthew could have quickly calculated her net worth based on a tithe of 10%. Jesus said, "That *is* her net worth." She has no pension and this meager amount would barely buy a dinner roll. The disciples would never have noticed what was so important to Jesus. She gave her last dime to God. Her gift is tender, desperate, and lavish. Jesus took notice. You see, he doesn't measure our gifts with a scale, but with a thermometer. After the offering is taken, we tend to count what was put in. God tends to count what was not. To that extent, this woman's gift was greater than all others that day.

This is a great story about giving. When read in context, however, it has broader ramifications. Both Mark and Luke sandwich this widow between the rebuke of the Pharisees and the cursing of the temple. In other words, the faithlessness of the leaders would ultimately result in the demise of the buildings. Their pomp and avarice is juxtaposed to the widow's simple, sacrificial faith. Again Jesus illustrates that in his upside-down kingdom it is the weak who are strong, the poor who are rich, and the humble who will be exalted. This kingdom holds precious promises for those who hold nothing else.

Further Reading: Deuteronomy 10:17-19; Psalm 146; 1 Timothy 5:3-16.

Ponderable Questions: Compare and contrast the widow with the Pharisees of the previous section. How does this widow's gift connect with the material that follows? Why are widows, along with children, the epitome of faithful disciples? How is money a clear barometer of our commitment to Christ?

Considerations for Prayer: "Guide me in pure and undefiled religion" (Jas. 1:27).

Premature Burial

{John 12:1-8; § 141}

Six days before the Passover, Jesus arrived at Bethany, where Lazarus lived, whom Jesus had raised from the dead. Here a dinner was given in Jesus' honor. Martha served, while Lazarus was among those reclining at the table with him. Then Mary took about a pint of pure nard, an expensive perfume; she poured it on Jesus' feet and wiped his feet with her hair. And the house was filled with the fragrance of the perfume. But one of his disciples, Judas Iscariot, who was later to betray him, objected, "Why wasn't this perfume sold and the money given to the poor? It was worth a year's wages." He did not say this because he cared about the poor but because he was a thief; as keeper of the money bag, he used to help himself to what was put into it. "Leave her alone," Jesus replied. "It was intended that she should save this perfume for the day of my burial. You will always have the poor among you, but you will not always have me."

Not more than two months ago Jesus had been in Bethany. He went to raise Lazarus from the dead. The whole village still reverberates with excitement. Lazarus and Jesus are back together again — something exciting is going to take place. Not only are the locals enthused, so are the pilgrims that followed Jesus from Jericho. They too have seen a miracle — Bartimaeus and his blind buddy both saw, shouted, and danced. Most of these devotees to Jesus are brand new followers. They just happened upon Jericho at the same time as Jesus when tens of thousands made their Passover pilgrimage to the Holy City. They are now just two miles away. Jesus hunkers down with a few close friends.

The host is Simon the Leper (Matt. 26:6). He's the only new player in this drama. All the others are familiar faces: Lazarus, Martha, Mary, and Judas. Each holds a special place in Jesus' heart and biography. As the meal begins, we're not surprised to find Mary at Jesus' feet. She's been there before (Luke 10:38-42). The last time she was listening, this time she's responding. No less than a half a dozen different times Jesus has clearly predicted his death in Jerusalem. This doesn't count his countless allusions to his substitutionary sacrifice. While Mary hardly understands the full implications of Jesus' death, she certainly knows that he's talked about it a lot. She knows that Jerusalem is a seedbed of fomenting political tension. She knows that Jesus is a wanted man, and this may be the last time she sees him. So, during this calm before the inevitable storm, she opens a pint of perfume resin. It is a costly gift worth a year's wages. Who knows how long she saved up for it or for what occasion she has saved it. One thing is certain, the only recipient of such a lavish gift was a corpse. Mary's anointing was standard burial practice. It is hard to know what's in her mind and heart, but her actions are clear enough.

The disciples no doubt protest her prediction of Jesus' death. The flash point for Judas, however, is the financial waste. Under the guise of compassion for the poor, Iscariot displays his avaricious greed. His disregard for Jesus is striking; he doesn't even consider the Master worthy of such a lavish gift. It will get worse. In fact, he will betray Jesus for much less — very much less. The others are ignorant of Iscariot's interior. His logic is compelling enough to rally the support of the eleven. His motives, however, are as self-centered as they can be.

In this story, John juxtaposed the most beautiful gift of Mary and the most selfish act of Judas. Here was a woman from a small town in Judea. She was not supposed to understand Jesus. But she did. On the other side is Judas, a well-connected Apostle. He was supposed to support Jesus. But he didn't. What is so interesting is that the Eleven couldn't tell which was on the right side of Jesus. Such is the nature of the Kingdom of God. The "in" are often ignorant, and the "out" are often nearest the Master's heart. The powerful can be avaricious while the sacrificial will ultimately be honored. Given their druthers, none of the Apostles would have chosen Mary's role over Judas's. In hindsight, however, she is clearly superior because she was inferior. She aligned herself with the death of Jesus, and, in so doing, tapped into his life. It was her sacrifice that became her greatest legacy. Her story is told to remind us today that the rules of the kingdom have not changed.

Further Reading: Matthew 26:6-13.

Ponderable Questions: Compare and contrast Iscariot and Mary. Do you think she really knew Jesus was about to die? What made this offering such a beautiful gift? What is so important about this story that it should be told wherever the gospel is preached (Matt. 26:13)? What lavish worship could you offer Jesus?

Considerations for Prayer: "Lord, lead me into lavish worship."

---

69 He Washed Their Feet 69

{John 13:1-5; § 145}

It was just before the Passover Feast. Jesus knew that the time had come for him to leave this world and go to the Father. Having loved his own who were in the world, he now showed them the full extent of his love. The evening meal was being served, and the devil had already prompted Judas Iscariot, son of Simon, to betray Jesus. Jesus knew that the Father had put all things under his power, and that he had come from God and was returning to God; so he got up from the meal, took off his outer clothing, and wrapped a towel around his waist. After that, he poured water into a basin and began to wash his disciples' feet, drying them with the towel that was wrapped around him.

We've just got to get da Vinci's painting out of our heads. The disciples did NOT walk single file into the room and sit down all on one side of the table for a photo. In fact, they probably shared a glass of wine with the hosts of the house before climbing the stairs to the upper room. When they entered, several conversations were bantered about the room. Most revolved around a single theme: "Which one of us is the greatest?"

This is a natural debate at a banquet because seating arrangements display the party's pecking order. Therefore, everyone wanted to get as close to the host as they could. It's kind of like the predictable and perpetual banter of children fighting for the front seat whenever the family goes to the mall. It was not an argument unique to the Twelve. Everyone who was anyone had engaged in the social jousting for chief seats.

What makes it so sickening on this particular occasion, however, is its juxtaposition to Jesus' passion. Within hours Jesus will lay down his life for them, and here they are still bickering like children over who sits where. Added to this, it is now the third time this same argument has been recorded. All three times the argument is preceded with Jesus' passion prediction. All three times it is followed by a pretty good tongue-lashing. This time, though, the rebuke is not audible, but visual.

While the Twelve are embroiled in controversy, Jesus strips down to the loincloth of a slave. He lays aside his garment to pick up a basin and towel. The argument at hand has left undone the menial duty of washing feet. It was the job of the lowest slave of the house to perform that duty. None of the Twelve will stoop so low. Jesus does. One by one they fall silent. Shocked, they watch with gaping mouths as the Master kneels, playing the role of a common slave. If they only knew how far he really descended in that moment. If they only knew how long he'd been playing that role!

Peter protests, "Lord, you'll *never* wash my feet!" "If I don't wash your feet," Jesus said, "you'll have no part with me." "Then give me a sponge bath," he replied. He's so impetuous. "No," Jesus responded, perhaps with a chuckle, "Just your feet need to be washed." One by one Jesus worked his way around the table — washing all twelve sets of feet. Perhaps I need to say it again, *washing **all** twelve sets of feet.* His love is radical and it extends even to traitors. Even now Jesus models for us a life of abandonment.

The basin and the towel are intimately connected with the cross. Both show Jesus' program for life. Rather than defending or promoting himself, he chose to lay down his life. His greatness is in his service, his power in his weakness, his gain in his loss, and his life in his death. This foot-washing episode is part of a larger paradigm, as is the cross. It is a new mode of existence, a new path to God. Instead of approaching God through human wisdom, strength, and self-promotion, Jesus blazed a new trail into this upside-down kingdom where the greatest are the least and the leaders are servants.

Notice that with both the foot washing and the cross there is a clarion call for his disciples to follow his lead. This is not something he did that we absorb and appreciate. It is a new pattern for us to follow, a new mode of existence which must mark our lives if we are to consider ourselves Christ's people. The cross and basin represent self-denial. They call us to trust God rather than promote ourselves, to serve, and if need be die for, others rather than protect our own interests.

There is a larger story here than just washing feet, and a larger stage than the Twelve. This lesson is a way of life, not an addendum to tack onto other reasonably moral behavior. It is not a prissy gesture of being nice to others. It is a subversive attack on worldly ethics of self-promotion and self-aggrandizement. It is the path of faith that trusts God to protect our interest and our honor. Unfortunately it is a lesson almost wholly lost in the church that stresses size, power, and prestige. This is the way of the world. The way of Jesus is the basin and a towel.

Further Reading: John 13:1-20; "Humility 2" — available in electronic form from College Press.

Ponderable Questions: How is the call to the basin and the towel identical to Jesus' demand that we carry a cross? If a group of Christians chose to live like this, how would it affect their marriages, families, church, and evangelism? How is this message subversive?

Considerations for Prayer: "Lord, teach me to be a rebel through self-abnegation."

He Descended from Greatness

{Matthew 26:21-25; § 146}

And while they were eating, he said, "I tell you the truth, one of you will betray me." They were very sad and began to say to him one after the other, "Surely not I, Lord?" Jesus replied, "The one who has dipped his hand into the bowl with me will betray me. The Son of Man will go just as it is written about him. But woe to that man who betrays the Son of Man! It would be better for him if he had not been born." Then Judas, the one who would betray him, said, "Surely not I, Rabbi?" Jesus answered, "Yes, it is you."

Words are inadequate to capture the emotions of this moment. Jesus is well aware of his impending death and imminent return to the Father. Torn between terror and glory, he looks around this table of Twelve. His heart nearly explodes at this strange medley of memories, love, sadness, pride, and disappointment. It was the sacred Passover meal, a pivotal moment in the annual cycle of his people. But this Seder was supremely unique — more charged than even the original Exodus. For this was the prelude to the focal point of all human history.

It would have been nice for Jesus to celebrate with unmitigated joy this one last meal with his faithful few. They've given so much to follow him; they've labored so diligently to believe in him. They really do deserve a respite before the storm now so close at hand. Unfortunately there is a bit of nasty business that must be settled. Like pawns on a chess board, all the players must take their places. Each actor must be cued to his mark on the stage — even the betrayer.

It has been a furious week of raging debates, clamoring crowds, aggressive enemies, and intense expectations. A three-year revolutionary tour is coming to a climax in the capital city. My how refreshing this meal must have been! For these few moments they hunker down in an upper room. The flickering flames of oil lamps bounce across the walls. They cast glows across thirteen intense faces. At one moment they reveal glimmering eyes and hopeful smiles. At other moments they expose furrowed brows and nervous questions.

Suddenly, Jesus drops a bombshell: one of you will betray me. Searching eyes dart around the room. Realizing there is no more likely candidate than themselves, this choral refrain echoes in the upper room: "Surely not I, Lord." Around the table each leans in heavily toward Jesus. Clamoring atop the others' questions, all yearn for Jesus to look them in the eye and say, "No, not you. Of course not you." In the commotion of the moment, none noticed Judas's question reduced "Lord" to "Rabbi." Nor did they notice Jesus' confirmation, "It is as you say."

It is not too surprising, really, that Judas went undetected. He most likely reclined at Jesus' back. With low tones, Jesus could have addressed Judas in a way that slipped by everyone else (with the possible exception of John). Likewise, when John leaned back on Jesus' breast and asked who it was, no one else could hear the reply except those three: "The betrayer is the one to whom I hand this bread." Judas took the morsel. As it entered his body, so did Satan. He slipped off into the night; the darkness was thick.

Two things about this incident are particularly striking. First, Jesus loved Judas. I don't mean necessarily that he had warm feelings toward him. What I mean is that Jesus extended himself to Judas to the bitter end. He was given the honor of the money bag, clean feet, the chief-seat next to Jesus, and even a heavenly throne. He forfeited it all. Why?! Our best guesses all come back to three biblical clues: Judas's love of money, God's sovereignty, and Satan's schemes. Somehow, these three are woven into Judas's defection. Regardless of the reason, Judas's betrayal flew in the face of Jesus' kindness. He had been highly honored. He deliberately descended.

Second, none of the others suspected Iscariot. He did the same miracles the others had. He preached the same sermons. He stayed up late around the campfire talking theology and telling jokes. He too had passion, vision, hopes, and fears. He was so like the others on the surface, yet damned to the core. How can it be that such a one would move in and out of the most elite group of disciples without detection? How can one say all the right words, do all the right things, even make all the right sacrifices, and still be the "Son of Perdition" (John 17:12)? Answer: His encounter with Christ never culminated in a relationship of love. Furthermore, the fact that God's sovereignty played a part in Judas's demise shouldn't cause us to criticize God. Rather, we should gratefully acknowledge that His sovereignty is woven deeply into the fabric of our own relationship with Jesus. We should celebrate God's choice that we were elected as vessels of honor, not pots for destruction. We should cringe at the thought that even Judas could weave in and out of Jesus' inner circle. If he was not so far from us, then perhaps we should be warned that we are not so far from him.

Further Reading: John 13:21-30; "Judas Iscariot" — available in electronic form from College Press.

Ponderable Questions: Why did Judas betray Jesus? What are some possible motives? Why did the disciples not suspect him? What does that tell us about being a follower of Jesus? How does God's sovereignty frighten and comfort you?

Considerations for Prayer: Read through Romans 9:10-26, giving thanks to God for his sovereign election and protection.

The Last Supper, the First Communion

{Matthew 26:26-29; § 148}

While they were eating, Jesus took bread, gave thanks and broke it, and gave it to his disciples, saying, "Take and eat; this is my body." Then he took the cup, gave thanks and offered it to them, saying, "Drink from it, all of you. This is my blood of the covenant, which is poured out for many for the forgiveness of sins. I tell you, I will not drink of this fruit of the vine from now on until that day when I drink it anew with you in my Father's kingdom."

For Jews, the Passover was not merely a memorial meal commemorating the past. It was an ongoing celebration of a nation in progress. It was roughly equivalent to our Independence Day, recounting the day when God's people became a nation. Thus, to "remember" at Passover, was not to passively imagine the days of yesteryear — the lore of yore. To "remember" meant to reenact, for they, too, were liberated by the powerful hand of God. There was an invisible and mystic thread that bound them to their forefathers. This Passover was the tangible evidence that the thread was real and intact.

Likewise, when Jesus bids his disciples "remember me," he is not charging us with a mental exercise. He is bidding us to reenact the great event of our spiritual Exodus, the very exodus the first one pointed to. Ours is the "real" exodus; ours is ultimate liberation. Moreover, ours is the greater nation. Just as the Egyptian Exodus was the genesis of a great nation, so the Golgotha Exodus instituted a greater kingdom. We are not merely a church which gathers to remember, we are a global kingdom that weekly reenacts our independence. In such a small tray, and with such fragile elements, is held an indissoluble and invisible thread which spans both the globe and the calendar. Christians of all brands and of all times are mystically bound to their Head through this memorial meal.

It is a strange meal with ancient roots. They reach all the way back to Jesus, the founder of our new nation. They even reach back to Moses, the founder of Israel. Yet the communion meal doesn't just connect us with the past. It connects us to the future. Jesus said, "I will not drink of this fruit of the vine from now on until that day when I drink it anew with you in my Father's kingdom." There was not just one cup of wine at the Passover meal, there were likely four. Luke mentions two of them, in fact. One before the breaking of the bread, and one after. Each of these cups were connected with one of four lines from Exodus 6:6-7a. The first cup was a prelude to the meal and probably was drunk before they ever got in the upper room. The second and third cups, connected with the communion, represented the freedom of Israel as well as her redemption. The fourth cup Jesus apparently never drank. It may still be waiting consumption. The last line of the Exodus text, connected with this fourth cup, says, "I will take you as my own people, and I will be your God."

In other words, the communion meal is not yet finished. When the king returns and the nation is consummated, we will finish the fourth cup. In essence, just as in the Jewish celebration of Passover, we don't have millions of individual celebrations, we have one elongated reenactment. We continue to remember; we continually reenact. And when he returns, we will finish the Eucharist with an eternal toast.

This mystic meal extends as far back as Moses and as far forward as eternity. Yet it also reaches above time into the heavenlies. This meal is more than symbolic. It is sacramental. That is to say, it doesn't merely represent something that happened a long time ago, it mirrors something happening in the spiritual realms even now. First Corinthians 10:16 says, " Is not the cup of thanksgiving for which we give thanks a participation in the blood of Christ? And is not the bread that we break a participation in the body of Christ?" Just as baptism reenacts on earth redemption in the heavenlies, so too the Lord's supper reenacts our communion with Christ. Through these tangible, transitory elements, we participate in the very body and blood of Jesus.

This meal looks outward to the body of Christ, inward to the Christian, upward as a sacrament, forward as a promise, and backward as a memorial. It is one of the grandest gifts Jesus ever gave. It is as broad as the world, older than the church, as high as the heavens, beyond space and time, and it all fits into a tiny tray on a communion table. It is packed into elements that fade as quickly as they're consumed yet endure unto eternity. Only Jesus could pull off a trick like that.

Further Reading: Exodus 6:6-7a; 1 Corinthians 10:16-22; 11:20-30.

Ponderable Questions: Do you believe this memorial is sacramental? How can we properly "remember" the Lord through this supper? How does this meal represent the founding of a new nation? How could we celebrate the Lord's Supper to make it more meaningful?

Considerations for Prayer: Celebrate the Lord's supper.

The Spirit Is Willing, the Flesh Is Weak

{Matthew 26:36-40; § 152}

Then Jesus went with his disciples to a place called Gethsemane, and he said to them, "Sit here while I go over there and pray." He took Peter and the two sons of Zebedee along with him, and he began to be sorrowful and troubled. Then he said to them, "My soul is overwhelmed with sorrow to the point of death. Stay here and keep watch with me." Going a little farther, he fell with his face to the ground and prayed, "My Father, if it is possible, may this cup be taken from me. Yet not as I will, but as you will." Then he returned to his disciples and found them sleeping. "Could you men not keep watch with me for one hour?" he asked Peter. "Watch and pray so that you will not fall into temptation. The spirit is willing, but the body is weak."

It must have felt strange to Jesus to enter this garden for the last time. Perhaps he felt like we do when we take one last walk through our empty house before we move. Memories cascade and tears flow. It is as if our history and future get compressed in the vice of one pregnant moment. Hope and fear, dreams and doubts collide.

This sliver of time is thick for Jesus. He passes by the tomb of Absalom in the valley of Kidron. Surely he pondered the similarities between David and himself, for it was Absalom's insurrection which chased the king from his city. It was on this very hill where David looked back over his shoulder and wept for Zion. Jesus had done that, too. On this hill he was hailed as king just four days earlier. From this spot on Tuesday afternoon he predicted the destruction of the city. From here he would ascend and to here he will return. It is a significant place and a colossal moment.

Here the suffering begins that will culminate on another hill, not so far away. These twin peaks of Gethsemane and Golgotha will punctuate the passion. Eight of his men Jesus leaves at the gate. Three he takes with him to the interior. There they sit, his closest friends, with this simple command: Pray. They fail — three times they fail and fall into temptation. So Jesus, a short distance away, was left alone. This is a trial he will have to face in isolation. He falls on his face and wrestles with God. "Father, if it is possible, let this cup pass from me." There are striking parallels between this prayer, John 17, and Hebrews 5:7 that surely betray the historic truth: Jesus wanted out. He pleaded for the cup of wrath to pass. He begged for an alternative path. Three times he prayed, three times the heavens echoed back with thunderous silence: NO, NO, NO.

The struggle of Jesus is so striking that some have tried to soften it. They suggest that he prayed not to avoid the cross, but to avoid a premature death right there in the garden. After all, they argue, Jesus said, "I'm sorrowful to the point of death." Moreover, to have Jesus beg off on the cross would make him less courageous than some other martyrs who have suffered without so much as a flinch. However, this vastly underestimates the difference between Jesus and a martyr. He is not dying for a cause he believes in. He is suffering for the sins of the world. His death is categorically different. Besides, his bravery is not measured by his feelings of fear, but by his resilient behavior. No, the text is clear; Jesus wanted out. Our eternity hung precariously in the balance while Jesus wrestled.

Ultimately God's will prevailed. For Jesus there is no other path. His final choice was made. He cast his lot with the likes of us, to become sin and die in our place. His tears and travail hearken back to another wilderness experience when he first chose this course. Like then, Luke says, the angels arrived to comfort the man of sorrows. He is not nearly as alone as it first appears. His weakness becomes resilience. His trudging in Gethsemane became a victory march on the *Via Dolorosa*.

Meanwhile, the disciples are asleep. Imagine that! Jesus wrestles, their salvation teeters in the balance, while they drool on a rock with their eyes rolled back in their heads. Had they only known how critical this moment was, had they seen Jesus' tears, his blood, the angels, perhaps then they would have remained awake. Maybe that's the crucial problem — perspective. Had they known what we know, surely they would have had the stoic resilience to forfeit sweet sleep. Ah, but there you have it. The spirit is willing but the flesh is weak. Are they really so different from us? Here we stand on the precipice of Jesus' second coming, drooling on rocks. The church is in her greatest days, oblivious to the Master's impending return. If we could only see our future as clearly as Peter's past, perhaps we could stay on task. The hour of prayer is not nearly as long when juxtaposed to eternity.

Further Reading: Matthew 26:41-46; Luke 22:39-46; John 17; Hebrews 5:7.

Ponderable Questions: What was it precisely that Jesus prayed for in the garden? God refused to answer Jesus' prayer. Can you think of other biblical giants whose petitions God refused to grant? What does that say about us when God says "no"? How could you adopt Jesus' perspective in prayer rather than Peter's?

Considerations for Prayer: Try to pray through John 17 and Matthew 26:36-40.

Betrayed . . . Arrested

{Luke 22:47-53; § 153}

While he was still speaking a crowd came up, and the man who was called Judas, one of the Twelve, was leading them. He approached Jesus to kiss him, but Jesus asked him, "Judas, are you betraying the Son of Man with a kiss?" When Jesus' followers saw what was going to happen, they said, "Lord, should we strike with our swords?" And one of them struck the servant of the high priest, cutting off his right ear. But Jesus answered, "No more of this!" And he touched the man's ear and healed him. Then Jesus said to the chief priests, the officers of the temple guard, and the elders, who had come for him, "Am I leading a rebellion, that you have come with swords and clubs? Every day I was with you in the temple courts, and you did not lay a hand on me. But this is your hour — when darkness reigns."

The drama of the arrest comes in three scenes, each devoted to a major player. Scene 1 begins when Jesus returns to the eight at the gate of the garden. Peter, James, and John follow a few steps behind. Their minds are still a bit groggy from their nap, but their eyes are now wide open for what they see. Emerging from the darkness is a familiar face, but it's in the wrong place. He should be standing with the Eleven. Instead he heads this company of soldiers some 600 strong. They are armed with torches, clubs, spears, and shields. They look like Pilate's troops, only they're led by the familiar faces of the Sanhedrin. It is such a strange mixture of persons.

According to John, Jesus is the first to speak, "Who are you looking for?" "Jesus of Nazareth," they reply. "I am he." With that they fell to the ground. They aren't just tongue-tied now, they're hog-tied — and that's a bad spot for a group of Jews! Jesus breaks the silence a second time; their response is the same. So the Master says, "I'm the one you're looking for. So why don't you let these others go?" With that Judas steps forward and confirms Jesus' confession with a kiss. Yet he is not the one in control of this moment, Jesus is. He asks, "Judas, are you really going to betray me with a kiss?" And he does.

In Scene 2 Peter steps forward. There is a quick flash — the reflection of the blade across the light of the torch. A man ducks quickly, shrieks in pain, and grabs the side of his head. He turns out to be Malchus, the High Priest's personal assistant. Peter told Jesus he would die with him. He now proves it. Outnumbered some 60 to 1, he's ready to go out in a blaze of glory as a martyr. To be sure, this is Peter's fate, but not just yet. Jesus intervenes. According to Matthew, he reminds Peter that he has 72,000 angels at his disposal should he care to use them. He heals Malchus with a touch. The evidence of Peter's assault disappears; so do the disciples. The hour is late and it is very dark.

In Scene 3 Jesus is treated like a common thug. His hands are tied, and he is led away to judgment. Nevertheless, he is the one who speaks, "Am I leading a rebellion, that you have come with swords and clubs? Every day I was with you in the temple courts, and you did not lay a hand on me. But this is your hour — when darkness reigns." They intend to put Jesus on trial. But before they ever get to Caiaphas's palace, Jesus accuses them. They, not he, will ultimately have to answer for their actions.

Three scenes, three players: Judas who betrays Jesus, the disciples who abandon him, and the chief priests who arrest him. Jesus speaks to each main character. His words to each are unique, yet to all three he says the same thing: I'm in charge here. Judas thought he was going to identify Jesus. Jesus beats him to the punch. Peter thought he was going to defend Jesus. Jesus winds up keeping him from being arrested. The Chief Priests intend to put him on trial. Yet before they leave the garden, Jesus is already casting the first accusation. He is in complete control of this entire scandalous affair. This we must not forget. Jesus died, not because of the treachery of Judas, the cowardice of the disciples, or the avarice of the leaders. He died because of a deliberate decision in the garden before any of these characters came on the scene. He died because of God's design and because of . . . well, because we too were in the garden. Our own sins loomed large there, along with those of the whole world. Each of us plays a part in the drama. However our particular scene is reenacted, this you should keep in mind — Jesus is in charge of that, too.

Further Reading: Acts 4:23-30; Psalm 2.

Ponderable Questions: What does this scene tell you about situations in your own life that seem to be spiraling out of control? Why was Jesus so troubled in the garden? What do you suppose went through his mind with each of these "players"? What perspective does Psalm 2 add to this scene in the garden?

Considerations for Prayer: Write a poem to God about this scene that includes these three players and Jesus' control.

---

74 Caught in the Courtyard 74

{Matthew 26:33-35,73-75; § 147 & 156}

Peter replied, "Even if all fall away on account of you, I never will." "I tell you the truth," Jesus answered, "this very night, before the rooster crows, you will disown me three times." But Peter declared, "Even if I have to die with you, I will never disown you." And all the other disciples said the same. . . . After a little while, those standing there went up to Peter and said, "Surely you are one of them, for your accent gives you away." Then he began to call down curses on himself and he swore to them, "I don't know the man!" Immediately a rooster crowed. Then Peter remembered the word Jesus had spoken: "Before the rooster crows, you will disown me three times." And he went outside and wept bitterly.

Have you ever been caught in the courtyard? Peter found himself there after slinking through the streets of Jerusalem, trailing the police escort. He came to Caiaphas's house, which was, of course, heavily guarded. John apparently knew the High Priestly family. His connections got Peter in. You can just imagine him looking around furtively. He's casing the joint to see if he and the boys can break Jesus out. Or at least he wants to overhear the strategic plan of the opposition. Either way, he is a spy, as skittish as a cat on a hot tin roof. (If that's not why he's there, I'm at a loss to figure out what Peter thinks he's doing in enemy territory!)

As he passes through the gate, he catches the sentry's eye. She was, typically, a teenager, up later than usual due to the hoopla. As Peter brushes past, she says, "Hey, I know you. You're one of those Galileans." She's just doing her job, but Peter's not impressed. "Shut up!" he says, "I don't know what you're talking about. *You* don't know what you're talking about." He leaves her at the gate and heads for the charcoal fire of the soldiers. She continues to stare. The embers illuminate his bundled face in hues of red and orange. The men around him are telling lively tales of a heroic capture. Peter, with everything in him, resists the urge to shout, "That's NOT what happened!"

After careful study the girl is sure it's him. She approaches the men and interrupts their banter. "This man is one of Jesus' disciples." They turn and glare. Peter protests, "I don't even know the man!" With that he moved back out to the gate. It was darker there, and nearer an exit. The trial in the courtyard is going no better than the one in the palace hall. The soldiers continue to stare. After careful consideration one of them says, "Yeah, I recognize the guy. He's the one that took a poke at Malchus, my relative." The group saunters over to Peter. For the third time they assert his affiliation with the Master. As the pressure builds, so does Peter's denial. With an oath he calls down curses on himself: "I swear to God I don't know the man!"

The darkness grew still. The crisp midnight air was pierced by the shrill cry of the cock. Two crows sent chills sprawling through Peter's soul. Across the courtyard, through the door, Jesus turns to catch Peter's eye. His look could have said so many things: "How could you?!" "I told you so!" "You impish jerk." But it was not a judgmental glare. It was simple sadness — pathos really. His look simply said, "I'm sorry . . . I'm sorry for you and I'm sorry for me." Peter ran into the night and wept bitterly.

Peter all but called Jesus a liar when he predicted his denial. Now he's faced with the harsh reality of his own failure. Have you ever been in the courtyard? Have you ever said to Jesus, "This is something I'll never do! Everyone else may be doing it, but not me!" Later you find yourself flat on your back, breathless, with your legs swept out from under you. Where does one go from the courtyard? Oh sure, there is a dark night of wailing. But that's not the end of Peter's story, nor of ours. The happy-sad news is that even for this Jesus died. The failure is not permanent any more than the penalty attached to it. Just as the courtyard and the cross go hand in hand, so do the resurrection and restitution. Live with it.

Further Reading: John 13:31-38; 18:15-18,25-27; Psalm 51.

Ponderable Questions: Why is it so hard sometimes to accept Christ's forgiveness for our sins? What appropriate steps can we take after we sin to be reconciled to a right relationship with God? What are some dangerous attitudes or ideas we must avoid in the process?

Considerations for Prayer: Confess your sins to God; receive his forgiveness and liberation.

Encounters with Christ

The Death and Resurrection of Christ

A Mock Trial

{Mark 14:55-65; § 155}

The chief priests and the whole Sanhedrin were looking for evidence against Jesus so that they could put him to death, but they did not find any. Many testified falsely against him, but their statements did not agree. Then some stood up and gave this false testimony against him: "We heard him say, 'I will destroy this man-made temple and in three days will build another, not made by man.'" Yet even then their testimony did not agree. Then the high priest stood up before them and asked Jesus, "Are you not going to answer? What is this testimony that these men are bringing against you?" But Jesus remained silent and gave no answer. Again the high priest asked him, "Are you the Christ, the Son of the Blessed One?" "I am," said Jesus. "And you will see the Son of Man sitting at the right hand of the Mighty One and coming on the clouds of heaven." The high priest tore his clothes. "Why do we need any more witnesses?" he asked. "You have heard the blasphemy. What do you think?" They all condemned him as worthy of death. Then some began to spit at him; they blindfolded him, struck him with their fists, and said, "Prophesy!" And the guards took him and beat him.

He was captured at night through the treachery of a friend — betrayed with a bribe. He is rushed into a kangaroo court in the middle of the night and accosted by false witnesses. Oh, surely they weren't blatant liars. But there's a whole lot more hearsay than evidence. There are no clear charges, and he is beaten as part of the interrogation. He is asked to incriminate himself, and the official body of leaders never actually voted for the verdict. They were led by a dominant high priest whose agenda was clear: this man must die for the welfare of the nation (John 11:49-53). Jesus' destiny was decided long ago.

The illegalities of the trial are striking. Nonetheless, we ought to meet the real Caiaphas, not merely the straw man erected in his image. Undoubtedly he loved his nation. Indeed, he was enmeshed in Roman politics. That's necessary to climb the ladder, you know. But even politicians have hearts. Surely he saw Jesus as a threat to national security, not just to his personal power. After all, a man that goes about turning over tables in the temple is bound to get noticed by Rome. Caiaphas is not far off. Jesus was wildly popular, prophetically intense, and although he was an uneducated Galilean, he really did have what it takes to start an uprising that would lead to massive bloodletting.

Caiaphas said, "The sooner he dies, the fewer Jews he would take with him." To this extent, he was right.

The first charge is threatening the temple. They hearken back to the words recorded in John 2, "Destroy this temple and I will raise it up again in three days." The problem is they misquoted him. Jesus never said *he* would destroy the temple, but *they* would. Oddly, they use this accusation against him at the very moment they are fulfilling his words. Because the witnesses can't get their stories straight, they are going to have to drop this first charge. You know what the funny thing is? It was actually a true charge — they just can't prove it. Jesus citation from Jeremiah 7:1-11 at the cleansing of the temple is highly suggestive of a Messianic remodeling which would require complete demolition. Furthermore, Mark's pairing of the cleansing of the temple with the cursing of the fig tree is also quite telling. Moreover, Matthew 24, spoken privately to the Apostles, is another incident where Jesus predicted the demise of the Holy City. They were actually right. Jesus did threaten the temple. He also carried through with it.

The second charge is blasphemy. That is, they accused him of reviling (or criticizing) God. "He never did that!" you say. True, he never came out and cursed God's name. However, in Jewish litigation, God could be cursed if you insulted him by arrogating yourself to his level. Jesus clearly did that. He claimed to be the Son of God and the Messiah of Israel. He claimed to have divine prerogative and power. He even went so far as to suggest that he could forgive sins and would soon sit at God's right hand until his enemies become his footstool. Oooh, that must have miffed Caiaphas. Here Jesus puts *him* on trial and threatens him in the name of Yahweh! No wonder the High Priest came uncorked. He tore his robe and shouted for a death sentence. If Jesus is not who he claims, then Caiaphas was absolutely right to kill him as a dangerous renegade. If Jesus is who he claims, however, they are about to make a galactic mistake.

Words begin to fly. Caiaphas goes into a tirade . . . something about defending the honor of God. The members of the Sanhedrin can't keep their seats. They alternate back and forth from shouting at Jesus to vociferous discussions among themselves. The soldiers begin to taunt, spit, and beat. The room is chaotic. Jesus stands alone, and he alone is silent. He answers not a single charge. Indeed, this fulfills Isaiah 53:5-7, "The LORD has laid on him the iniquity of us all."

In a number of ways, Caiaphas was exactly right. Unfortunately, his misperception of Jesus made him dead wrong. As was so often the case in the life of Christ, the only question that really mattered was the one concerning his identity. If you are right in all other issues, but you get this one wrong, colossal tragedy is inevitable.

Further Reading: Isaiah 53.

Ponderable Questions: What questions did Caiaphas get right? How do men like that get caught in such a tangled web of deceit and injustice? Is the identity of Jesus really the central question to Christianity? How so? What happens when people get his identity wrong?

Considerations for Prayer: Thank Jesus for taking your sins in his suffering.

---

76 A Mockery of Justice 76

{John 18:28-31; 19:1-6; § 159 & 161}

Then the Jews led Jesus from Caiaphas to the palace of the Roman governor. By now it was early morning, and to avoid ceremonial uncleanness the Jews did not enter the palace; they wanted to be able to eat the Passover. So Pilate came out to them and asked, "What charges are you bringing against this man?" "If he were not a criminal," they replied, "we would not have handed him over to you." Pilate said, "Take him yourselves and judge him by your own law." "But we have no right to execute anyone," the Jews objected. . . . Then Pilate took Jesus and had him flogged. The soldiers twisted together a crown of thorns and put it on his head. They clothed him in a purple robe and went up to him again and again, saying, "Hail, king of the Jews!" And they struck him in the face. Once more Pilate came out and said to the Jews, "Look, I am bringing him out to you to let you know that I find no basis for a charge against him." When Jesus came out wearing the crown of thorns and the purple robe, Pilate said to them, "Here is the man!" As soon as the chief priests and their officials saw him, they shouted, "Crucify! Crucify!"

Pilate was Rome's legate over Palestine with the power of life and death. He held court early that morning, knowing that one important case would fill his docket. A certain peasant rebel from Galilee had been captured the night before. The Jewish leaders escorted him to the Praetorium. Their persnickety piety wouldn't allow them to enter, but wouldn't hinder them from corruption either. Pilate's immediate impulse was to proclaim his innocence. In fact, Pilate will attempt more than a half a dozen times to let him go. Three times he says bluntly, "I find no fault in him." Once he tried to pawn him off on Herod, another time he tried to substitute Barabbas, he even tried to wash his blood-stained hands. This pesky problem just won't go away. Herod returns him, his enemies hound him, his followers abandon him. Yet there he stands, noble, silent — the epitome of truth.

Suddenly the governor, like Annas and Caiaphas earlier, finds himself on trial rather than Jesus. It is clear that he was innocent, given over merely for envy. Pilate wants to release him in the worst way, but his clients threaten to blackmail him in Rome. Here is his dilemma: Jesus' life or my career? He delivers him over to the executioner to save his own petty political career (which will end prematurely in just three years when he will be banished to Gaul). Don't be too hard on Pilate. Some of us have sold him out for much less.

The soldiers flog him. This involves stripping the victim, tying him to a wall or a post, and then flaying his back with a whip. This particular instrument likely had 5-9 leather strands tethered to a wooden handle and imbedded with either lead balls or sheep bones. At first it would merely lacerate the epidermis. As the wounds swelled with fluid, the tissue would become soft and eventually tear deep into the subcutaneous tissue. Vertebrae were exposed: back, buttocks, thighs, and chest were flayed. The Jews limited their lashings to 40 (Deut 25:3). Unfortunately, these are Romans with no such restrictions. Six of every ten men died from such scourging alone, some from loss of blood, others from the loss of their entrails.

A crown of thorns was woven and placed, not so gingerly, on his brow. Jesus winced; blood flowed. Soldiers' spittle dripped from his beard after a mock coronation. His abdomen throbbed from gut punches. His ears rang from the staff slapped against it. The purple soldier's cape began to crust over with coagulated blood and stick to the fibers of his open lacerations — that is, until they ripped it from his flesh to parade him through the city streets. Still Jesus remained silent, except for the sporadic yelps of agony.

Standing there, swollen and bloody, he didn't look much like a conquering king. Some victorious Messiah! The Romans disdained him. The Jews railed against him. His own followers abandoned him. It looked like God had too. Jesus stands alone — very much alone. If he is who he claimed, then this is the greatest disguise of all human history. It is no small wonder the crowds call for his execution. Many who surrounded the Praetorium that day would be supporters of the Sanhedrin. Their colors are clear. Even those who used to honor Jesus see him now in a different light. He is no victorious liberator. He must be a fraud, a dangerous revolutionary who leads people astray. What else do you do with a heretic, an impostor, and a blasphemer?! Pilate brings his pummeled body out to the crowd and says, "Behold the man." The people cried with one undulated voice, *"Crucify Him, Crucify Him!"* So Pilate did . . . for them . . . for us too.

Further Reading: John 18:28–19:16; Luke 23:1-6,13-25.

Ponderable Questions: What charges are brought against Jesus before Pilate? Which did he investigate and what did he find? List the physical suffering that Jesus has endured up to this point. Why did God have Jesus stand before Roman authorities? What do you suppose went through Pilate's mind as he wrestled with Jesus' identity and innocence?

Considerations for Prayer: Find a picture of Jesus that represents his beating at this trial. Use it to help you meditate on Christ's suffering.

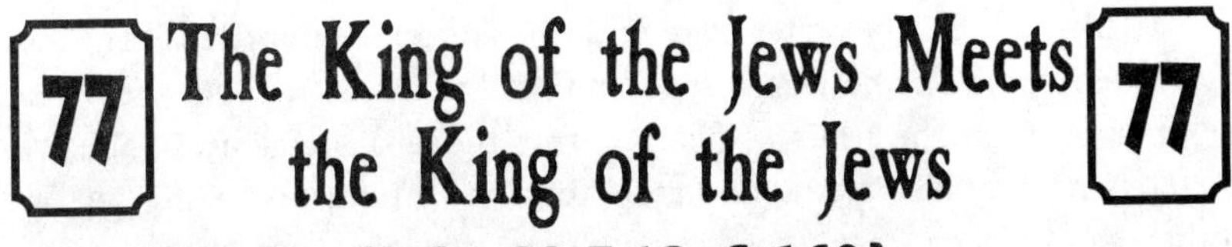

77 The King of the Jews Meets the King of the Jews 77

{Luke 23:7-12; § 160}

When he learned that Jesus was under Herod's jurisdiction, he sent him to Herod, who was also in Jerusalem at that time. When Herod saw Jesus, he was greatly pleased, because for a long time he had been wanting to see him. From what he had heard about him, he hoped to see him perform some miracle. He plied him with many questions, but Jesus gave him no answer.

> The chief priests and the teachers of the law were standing there, vehemently accusing him. Then Herod and his soldiers ridiculed and mocked him. Dressing him in an elegant robe, they sent him back to Pilate. That day Herod and Pilate became friends — before this they had been enemies.

Jesus has never met Herod, but the readers of Luke have — several times. We met him when he beheaded John the Baptist, all because of a drunken promise to his teenage step-daughter whose lewd dance delighted his perverted dinner guests. We met him again when he confessed Christ to be a mysterious miracle worker with the power of the beheaded Baptist. Another time we learned that he wanted to meet the Master. Some Pharisees warned Jesus about his intentions, and Jesus called him an insignificant she-fox. The general tenor of these Herod texts is that Herod is dying to meet Jesus and Jesus will likely die if he does.

Herod Antipas is only one of the four Herods of Luke's two volumes. The first is Herod the Horrible (or "the Great" according to some). He tried to "meet" Jesus too, but his parents stole him away to Egypt. The other baby boys of Bethlehem were not so fortunate. The second is Herod Antipas, already mentioned — the murderer of Jesus' forerunner and friend. The third is Herod Agrippa of Acts 12. He is the one who killed the first apostolic martyr. Under his cruel devices James lost his head and Peter only narrowly escaped. From these first three we learn that whenever Jesus or his associates stand before a Herod they die.

The last Herod was Agrippa II. Paul stood trial before him in Acts 25 & 26. This is an interesting parallel to Jesus' trial. On both occasions the Herods proclaimed the innocence of their captives and yet didn't let them go. Both Jesus and Paul were sent on to Roman legislators. Jesus died immediately before Pilate. Paul will also eventually die before Nero. The similarities are striking.

Luke is the only writer to record this Herod encounter. Clearly he is drawing parallels between Jesus and Paul in his Gospel and Acts. He is showing that the trials of Jesus mirror those of Peter and Paul. By extension, they also give us a model to follow in our own suffering. In other words, what Jesus goes through, we can also expect to endure. How he handles himself is a pattern for our own action. Most striking along this line is Jesus' silence. He chose not to defend himself, like a lamb before its shearers (Isa 53:7). The king of the Jews refused to talk to the king of the Jews. He chose faith in God above personal vindication. This may not mean that we never speak out on our own behalf.

But it certainly means that the pattern of our lives is faith in God rather than manipulation for our own advantage.

There is one other lesson that surfaces from this story. In both Paul's and Jesus' trials before Herod, there was great pomp and circumstance. Herod is surrounded by nobles, robes, and clout. Yet in the end, it was Jesus and Paul, not Herod, who was most memorable. The very introduction to this essay is necessary because very few today remember the Herods. Jesus and Paul, however, are globally famous. These nobles would be scandalized today to realize how little their lives are remembered, particularly compared to these peasants they tried. The lesson is clear. It is Jesus and his people who are the most regal. It matters very little what kinds of clothes they wear, crowns that adorn them, crowds that surround them, or power they wield. The people of God are the real royalty in Yahweh's eternal economy. If we follow Jesus, we will encounter Herod. Remember who you are.

Further Reading: Luke 3:19-20; 9:7-9; 13:31-33; Acts 12:1-6,19-23.

Ponderable Questions: Trace the four Herods of Luke and Acts. How did they treat Jesus and his followers? Do these incidents give us any guidelines for how we should respond to our enemies? What lessons do they teach about the resilience and dignity of the church?

Considerations for Prayer: Tell Jesus what you feel about his regal dignity.

78 The Death of Life 78

{John 19:17-19,30; § 164-165}

Carrying his own cross, he went out to the place of the Skull (which in Aramaic is called Golgotha). Here they crucified him, and with him two others—one on each side and Jesus in the middle. Pilate had a notice prepared and fastened to the cross. It read: JESUS OF NAZARETH, THE KING OF THE JEWS. . . . When he had received the drink, Jesus said, "It is finished." With that, he bowed his head and gave up his spirit.

John says it so simply: "They crucified him." No gruesome photographs, no wrenching videos. No blood bespattered across the papyrus, just the smallest drop of ink to describe the centerpiece of all human history. As Peter says, they killed the author of life (Acts 3:15). One must ponder these words to grasp just how desperately sad and damning they are. God visited us one day, and we executed him ruthlessly. The dastardly defection that began at Eden is now complete.

The sign simply read, "King of the Jews." It was supposed to be a criminal charge. It turned out to be the only honest words of the trial. This modest statement stands in stark contrast to the scene that surrounds it. The king of kings was killed between two common thieves. Towering over the city of God, he died.

The cross is such a simple symbol. It is easy to adorn — a thing of beauty when plated with gold. It fits nicely in our churches, at least after it's been polished. What a paradox! The very object of scorn has become our symbol of success. The epitome of defeat has been emblazoned on warriors' shields. Even after Paul said that it was a stumbling block to the Jews and foolishness to Greeks (1 Cor. 1:23), the church still clung tenaciously to the cross. Why?!

The Romans knew well the excruciating physical realities of the cross. They were expert executioners who knew precisely where to place the nails to maximize suffering. They were equipped with iron mallets to break their victims' legs and lances to probe for vestiges of life. This powerful political tool had checked dozens of revolutionary movements at the cost of thousands of lives.

The Jews, on the other hand, knew of the severe social consequences of the cross. They understood that Romans only crucified foreign rebels and the worst villains of their own people. To hang on a cross meant that you were a failed revolutionary or a scalawag of the most despicable sort. Not only were you an enemy of the empire and an embarrassment to your race, you were cursed by God himself (Deut. 21:23; Gal. 3:13).

The Romans knew its physical consequences, the Jews its social ones. So our question stands: under such circumstances, why did Christians appropriate the cross as their dominant symbol? After all, they could have used the dove, a shepherd, or the ΙΧΘΥΣ. The answer is this: beyond its physical and social implications, the church understood well the *spiritual* implications of the cross. It was at the cross that we had our sins forgiven. We were ransomed from hell at a very high price (Mark 10:45). Moreover, it was in this horrid act that the Lordship of Jesus was eternally established (Ps. 118:22, 24). In that, we can't help but rejoice. But it is bigger still. It was here that the deadly dragon, the Devil himself, was ultimately defeated (Rev. 12:9-12). He was stripped of his power to accuse as he was hurled from heaven. The gates of his hellish abode were crushed by the frontal assault of the Word Incarnate. As he passed through Hades (cf. 1 Pet. 3:19-20), Jesus defeated our greatest enemy. Death is now but a vapor, no longer the viper with a poisonous bite (1 Cor. 15:54-57). Amazingly, the cross is bigger still, for its work is not yet finished. Our very souls were redeemed that day. Our bodies, however, have yet to taste the incredible power of the cross. The power of the cross will one day transform our physical form into an imperishable body like Christ's (1 Cor. 15:42-49). In fact, not only will our bodies be transformed, the earth itself will be renewed (Rom. 8:18-21).

The cross changes *everything* — literally! It stands not only as the symbol of Christianity, but as the centerpiece of all human history. It is the lens through which all cosmic history is viewed, past, present and future. It is the ground on which we stand and the very breath we breathe. Perhaps it will take eternity to appreciate just how huge are these six words which begin and end this pericope: "They crucified him. . . . It is finished."

Further Reading: John 19:20-30; Luke 23:26-49; Matthew 27:32-56; "Theology of the Cross" — available in electronic form from College Press.

Ponderable Questions: Why was the cross necessary? List all the things that will be accomplished because of the cross. What does it mean that Jesus died for you? How can we die with him (Gal. 2:20)?

Considerations for Prayer: Memorize 2 Corinthians 5:21.

79 There's Just Something about the Way He Said My Name 79

{John 20:14-18; § 173}

She turned around and saw Jesus standing there, but she did not realize that it was Jesus. "Woman," he said, "why are you crying? Who is it you are looking for?" Thinking he was the gardener, she said, "Sir, if you have carried him away, tell me where you have put him, and I will get him." Jesus said to her, "Mary." She turned toward him and cried out in Aramaic, "Rabboni!" (which means Teacher). Jesus said, "Do not hold on to me, for I have not yet returned to the Father. Go instead to my brothers and tell them, 'I am returning to my Father and your Father, to my God and your God.'" Mary Magdalene went to the disciples with the news: "I have seen the Lord!"

Have you ever been blinded by grief? So sorrowful that you can't even see straight? Then you know how Mary feels right now. This is the only man who truly loved her. He released her from seven demons and gave her a new lease on life. She had followed him faithfully to the bitter end. Long after the men defected, she stayed by his side. While they hid, she wailed. Even now, three days after his death, she comes to pay homage — as if a corpse cared.

It had been a long morning already. Before the eastern sky gave way to dawn, she meticulously prepared spices. She, along with several other women, was determined to give their master a proper burial. Indeed, Joseph of Arimathea had lavished some seventy-five pounds of perfume on his body. But Joseph didn't know Jesus like they did; he couldn't possibly love Jesus as they had. With measured steps through dim and narrow streets, they discuss how they could move the stone. Undoubtedly the guards wouldn't mind their offering, but they certainly wouldn't tamper with Pilate's seal.

When they arrive at the garden, their question about the stone becomes irrelevant. It has been rolled away, and the guards are gone. So too is Jesus' body. The women are devastated. That is, until two men dressed in white proclaim the good news that Jesus is alive. Perhaps Mary takes off before these angels make their announcement to the other women. Or perhaps her grief makes her deaf to their words. Either way, she runs off in grief and disbelief. She informs John and Peter of the situation. John outruns Peter to the tomb; they both beat Mary. By the time she arrives, they have already investigated the scene. As they head home, they brush by her with little or no acknowledgment. Such was the status of women in her day. She stands paralyzed. Her stomach is in knots, her eyes filled with tears.

The angels appear again. She mistakes them for gardeners. This is somewhat strange since they are dressed in white. Apparently she is not thinking clearly. The angels ask, "Why are you crying?" This question, to Mary, must seem absurd. "They have taken my Lord away," she said, "and I don't know where they have put him." Of course, Mary's tears, to the angels, must seem absurd. Jesus is alive as he promised, and this silly woman is moping around the tomb!

Before they can answer, Jesus appears. He repeats the angel's question, "Why are you crying?" Mary mistakes Jesus for the gardener. She begs for an inside scoop on where they have taken the corpse. Then Jesus calls her name, "Mary." There was just something about the way he said her name. Perhaps it was his tenderness, perhaps some inflection. Her eyes open, her heart fills. Mary lunges at Jesus in one grand moment of recognition. She clings to him for dear life. And that's exactly what he is. Jesus, however, sends her on her way. There are others who need to know.

Why would the Gospel writers highlight this appearance? For one thing, it was the first. That is part of what makes it most extraordinary. After all, women, in Jesus' day didn't have much status. The fact that Jesus appears to a woman first indicates that we are dealing with a historical event. After all, no writer of fiction would have started the witness of Jesus with a woman. Furthermore, Jesus honors Mary, a woman and ex-demoniac. If she is welcome, everyone else is too.

Yet there is something more. Mary's experience is a mirror of our own. Through sorrow and tears, Jesus appears. In spite of prophetic predictions and sometimes even angels, we just can't see him. Then, when all hope is gone, Jesus calls our name. His voice pierces the dark night of our soul, and we lunge at him. Clinging for dear life, we feel his nail-scarred hands pry our fingers off his feet. He sends us on our way with a commission, for there are others who yet need to know he is alive.

Further Reading: I Corinthians 15; "Resurrection Appearances" — available in electronic form from College Press.

Ponderable Questions: What must have been going through the mind and hearts of the angels, Mary, and Jesus? Have you experienced a dark night of the soul in which Jesus appeared to you? What are the implications of the resurrection of Jesus for the Christian? What does Jesus' resurrection tell us about our own future resurrection?

Considerations for Prayer: Lord Jesus, be as real and present to me as you were to Mary.

80 We Weary Travelers 80

{Luke 24:13-16,25-27,32-25; § 176-177}

Now that same day two of them were going to a village called Emmaus, about seven miles from Jerusalem. They were talking with each other about everything that had happened. As they talked and discussed these things with each other, Jesus himself came up and walked along with them; but they were kept from recognizing him. . . . He said to them, "How foolish you are, and how slow of heart to believe all that the prophets have spoken! Did not the Christ have to suffer these things and then enter his glory?" And beginning with Moses and all the Prophets, he explained to them what was said in all the Scriptures concerning himself. . . . They got up and returned at once to Jerusalem. There they found the Eleven and those with them, assembled together and saying, "It is true! The Lord has risen and has appeared to Simon." Then the two told what had happened on the way, and how Jesus was recognized by them when he broke the bread.

Their steps, like their conversation, are sullen but deliberate. They return home to Emmaus after the Passover in Jerusalem. It was a high and holy feast, pregnant with hope but punctuated with despair. Cleopas and his friend had never been more hopeful for the Messiah — never more sure. Yet dreams can wither; hopes can be dashed. They return with bowed heads and broken hearts.

Their duet becomes a trio as a stranger joins them. He inquired about their heaviness. They were appalled at his apparent ignorance.

How could anyone not know what just happened in their capital city. Little did they know that it was they who were ignorant, not he. They didn't know that it was Jesus. Nor did they know how he truly fulfilled their dreams and expectations. They did not know the messianic passages nor the power of the resurrection.

For the remainder of their seven-mile trek, Jesus opened their eyes to the Scriptures. When they arrived, they compelled him to stay. At supper he opened their eyes to himself. He took the loaves in his hands, assuming the posture of the patron of the house. He prayed and broke the bread. Something in his manner (or was it in his prayer?), exposed the *déja vu.* Suddenly they saw him. Their hearts raced, trying to keep up with their minds. "If Jesus is alive, then he is the Messiah, only of a different sort than we imagined. What does this mean to the kingdom? We must tell the others." Then, in an instant, he vanishes. They don't know where he went or how. One thing is certain, however; they made better time getting back to Jerusalem than they did to Emmaus.

This appearance is bigger than it first seems. There is much symbolism here: Two legal witnesses, a journey of faith, veiled sight, sorrow turned to joy, and fulfilled prophecy. It is the quintessential resurrection appearance. It is also the biography of a disciple. Somewhere along our journey Jesus shows up. We don't know just who he is. But as the curtains lift, our hearts begin to burn. Then suddenly, mysteriously, we see him. We don't know what it all means, but we know that the world will never again be the same. With frantic feet and panting breath, we race to tell all who will listen that we have discovered Jesus — and that he is alive!

Further Reading: Luke 24:13-32; "Theology of the Resurrection" — available in electronic form from College Press.

Ponderable Questions: What elements in this story could be symbolic of our own discipleship? How did they finally recognize Jesus? At what times in your life have you come to a sudden realization of Jesus' presence and reality? How can we help others realize that Jesus is alive?

Considerations for Prayer: Share in a communion service. Ask Jesus to show himself through the fellowship of breaking bread.

81 He Came to His Own; They Believed Him Not 81

{John 20:19-22; § 178-179}

On the evening of that first day of the week, when the disciples were together, with the doors locked for fear of the Jews, Jesus came and stood among them and said, "Peace be with you!" After he said this, he showed them his hands and side. The disciples were overjoyed when they saw the Lord. Again Jesus said, "Peace be with you! As the Father has sent me, I am sending you." And with that he breathed on them and said, "Receive the Holy Spirit. If you forgive anyone his sins, they are forgiven; if you do not forgive them, they are not forgiven."

Somehow he appears though locked doors. Jesus greets his disciples with the standard Jewish "Shalom." They just about freak. He proves it's himself with his hands and side. They believe.

We're never told why, but Thomas was absent. You can imagine the earful he got when he returned. Wild with joy, they share every last detail. He's not buyin' it! Perhaps he muttered, "Dead men don't rise." Undoubtedly the disciples expend no little effort trying to convince him otherwise.

A week later to the day it happens again. Same song, second verse. In fact, Jesus uses the exact same words. His greeting is identical. And his command to Thomas is nearly a quotation from Thomas's own words a week before! "Put your finger here in my hands and your fist in my side." There is no argument now. Thomas believes. Indeed, he crosses a serious Jewish line by declaring Jesus to be his God.

No one would argue that a resurrection is hard to swallow. That's why Jesus went to great lengths to predict it (Matt. 12:40; 16:21; 17:9; 17:22-23; 20:18-19; 26:32; Mark 14:28; John 2:19-22). Then he proved it by appearing to key witnesses, eating the fish, and letting Thomas touch him. He wanted there to be no doubt that he was alive. Jesus wants more, however. He wasn't merely eradicating doubt, he was building faith. After all, at some point the appearances would stop. Then there must be a new breed of disciple. She would believe based on valid testimony, not existential experience. Her foundation would be a canonical witness, not a personal encounter. As wonderful as encounters are, they are easily misinterpreted and poorly remembered. Jesus is wise to push his disciples to the next level of faith.

Verses 22-23 is the Apostles' personal Pentecost. Here Jesus breathes on them and promises the Holy Spirit. Some see this as a preview of coming attractions. Others believe it is the point at which the Apostles appropriated the person and power of the Holy Spirit. However, this theological question is merely one of chronology. Regardless of *when* they received the Holy Spirit, the important thing is that the power of God would reside in them to declare the forgiveness of sins (cf. Matt. 16:19; 18:18-20). Obviously the Apostles played a special role in the church. They established the church and instituted Christian doctrine. In other words, they were the first to preach Christ and the last to establish the parameters of our faith. Even so, every Spirit-filled believer receives this selfsame commission. All disciples are to offer forgiveness of sins to the world (2 Cor. 5:18-20). This is not merely an issue of apologetics. Through the resurrection, the witnesses of Jesus assure believers that their sins are forgiven.

The point of this passage is not Thomas's doubt but our own proclamation. He was the watershed between existential faith and documented evidence. According to verses 30-31, we continue to persuade men through this ancient testimony. We continue this phenomenal offer of the forgiveness of sins. Doubting Thomases abound. If they could just believe this report, they could develop true faith in the living Christ. Then they could believe their sins are forgiven. Then they would confess with Thomas, "My Lord and my God."

Further Reading: John 20:19-31.

Ponderable Questions: How is Thomas the watershed between biblical disciples and us who believe without seeing? Why is faith without sight important and superior to faith based on sight? How is it that we, today, have the power to proclaim someone else's sins forgiven (cf. 2 Cor. 5:18-20)? Are we doing a very good job of this?

Considerations for Prayer: Simply tell Jesus what you believe about him.

82 Do You Love Me? 82

{John 21:6-7,9,13-15; § 180}

He said, "Throw your net on the right side of the boat and you will find some." When they did, they were unable to haul the net in because of the large number of fish. Then the disciple whom Jesus loved said to Peter, "It is the Lord!" As soon as Simon Peter heard him say, "It is the Lord," he wrapped his outer garment around him (for he had taken it off) and jumped into the water. . . . When they landed, they saw a fire of burning coals there with fish on it, and some bread. . . . Jesus came, took the bread and gave it to them, and did the same with the fish. This was now the third time Jesus appeared to his disciples after he was raised from the dead. When they had finished eating, Jesus said to Simon Peter, "Simon son of John, do you truly love me more than these?" "Yes, Lord," he said, "you know that I love you." Jesus said, "Feed my lambs."

So much of this scene is *déja vu*. The disciples have returned to Galilee where it all began. More than that, they are back in their boats. They fish all night — and catch nothing. A lone figure stands on the shore. From a hundred yards away he shouts, "Have you caught any fish?" An admission of failure is always difficult for fishermen. "Throw your nets on the other side," came the response. It was a stupid suggestion, followed only by sheer desperation or instinctive obedience.

It was a whale of a catch! John's eyes widened. He remembered the last time this happened. It was more than two years ago, the very day they traded their nets for pulpits. John blurts out, "It is the Lord!" Once again John is the first to understand, and Peter is the first to respond. He throws his fishing jacket around him and dives into the lake. He swims to Jesus while his partners manhandle this awkward squirming bundle trailing behind their boat.

There are no words recorded between Jesus and Peter. Perhaps none passed. After all, what do you say to the one you denied? This was the third time Peter saw Jesus. Perhaps he's still stymied.

The boat, the catch, the call — it is all so pregnant with meaning. But nothing was quite so reminiscent that day as the charcoal fire and the broken bread. Both are poignant reminders of Peter's greatest failure. After breakfast came his greatest fear. It's time to talk about it.

Jesus takes him aside and asks, "Simon, do you love me?" Not only does Jesus' question pierce his soul, so does the name he uses. Did he have to use Peter's pre-apostolic name? Had he fallen so far? Not once, not twice, but three times this question bombarded his soul. As painful as it was, he knew he had it coming — once for each denial. Yet even in his discipline, Jesus is kind. The one who brashly claimed to love Jesus "more than these," was reinstated as the rock. The others watched — all doubts were dispelled.

This *déja vu* creeps along the calendar to our own time. The scene refuses to sit passively in Peter's boat. The faces change and time marches on, but that solitary figure still stands on the edge of the lake. Illumined by a charcoal fire, he's still prepared to distribute the broken bread. We receive it from his hands. Like Peter, in the presence of our peers, we are reinstated as fishers of men. The words still echo: "Do you love me? . . . Feed my sheep!" It seems significant that at least one of these Gospels ends, not with Jesus' resurrection, but with Peter's restoration.

Further Reading: John 21:1-25.

Ponderable Questions: Have you ever felt like Peter did — that there was no use for you in the kingdom? How does this text relate to that experience of yours? If you could erase your painful past, what would you dream of doing for God? Is it still possible for you to be used to feed God's sheep?

Considerations for Prayer: "Lord, show me the sheep you would have me feed."

Finish It!

{Matthew 28:18-20; § 181}

All authority in heaven and on earth has been given to me. Therefore go and make disciples of all nations, baptizing them in the name of the Father and of the Son and of the Holy Spirit, and teaching them to obey everything I have commanded you. And surely I am with you always, to the very end of the age.

Words that pass through dying lips are momentous. They come from the deepest places of the heart. Jesus' words here come from that same place. From his deepest passions spring this mandate. As he ascended to heaven, he cared for nothing more than global conquest. He is not so interested in establishing a church as he is in founding a kingdom. He desires every man, woman, and child from every nation, tongue, and tribe to hear this marvelous message. Their sins can be forgiven; their souls can run free.

Oddly, he left this grand task, his *magnum opus*, in the hands of a dozen indigent peasants. They were ill-equipped, save the power of the Holy Spirit. Yet, like mustard seed, this kingdom message slowly, sometimes imperceptibly, permeated nations. It crept like leaven across the surface of our planet. It has been persecuted and ostracized, criticized and ignored. Yet its relentless advance is unquestionable. The kingdom of Christ dominates much of this earth. To call it the most populous religion is trifling, though not inaccurate.

Still, there is much work to do. Approximately 20% of the peoples of this earth have yet to hear the name of our Lord Jesus, let alone have a saving encounter with the Christ. That is, a billion people are lost, with little hope of hearing the message of salvation. Scores of languages have not a scrap of Scripture. Many national borders are closed to missionaries. This commission of Christ can no longer be the vision of a few radicals. It has to become the heartbeat of the kingdom. It must become the marching orders of every disciple who has had an encounter with Christ. How dare we claim to love Jesus, how dare we address him as Lord, and not pick up the final gauntlet he laid down before us. This is not optional — it is what he caressed with his final breath.

This is our commission, but it is *his* mission. Jesus *will* complete his purpose of redeeming this whole world. Then he will return. This is beyond question. The only uncertainty is where he will find *you* upon his return. Will your hands be folded or sweaty? We who have had an encounter with Christ have been wrenched from passive observation and thrust into frenzied participation. Could Jesus say but one word to his church on the dawn of this new millennium, surely the last he spoke would echo across time to shatter our complacency. Surely he would shout: FINISH IT!

Further Reading: Mark 16:15-20; John 20:21-23; Acts 1:7-8; "Our Commission" — available in electronic form from College Press.

Ponderable Questions: What are we doing currently to proclaim Jesus' kingdom to all the world? What could we do better? Is it realistic to think that we could actually complete this commission in our lifetime?

Considerations for Prayer: "Lord, help me finish what you started."

List of Supplemental Studies

Essential Readings in the Life of Christ

Aland, Kurt. *Synopsis of the Four Gospels.* United Bible Society, 1972.

Brown, Raymond E. *The Birth of the Messiah: A Commentary on the Infancy Narrative.* Garden City, NY: Doubleday, 1977.

_______________. *The Death of the Messiah: From Gethsemane to the Grave: A Commentary on the Passion Narrative in the Four Gospels.* New York: Doubleday, 1994.

Bruce, F.F. *The Hard Sayings of Jesus.* Downers Grove, IL: InterVarsity, 1983.

Edersheim, Alfred. *The Life and Times of Jesus the Messiah.* McLean, VA: Macdonald, 1883.

Ferguson, Everett. *Backgrounds of Early Christianity.* Grand Rapids: Eerdmans, 1987.

Foster, R.C. *Studies in the Life of Christ.* Joplin, MO: College Press, 1995.

Green, Joel B., Scot McKnight, and I.H. Marshall. *Dictionary of Jesus and the Gospels.* Downers Grove, IL: InterVarsity, 1992.

Linnemann, Eta. *Is There a Synoptic Problem?* Grand Rapids: Baker, 1992.

Manning, Brennan. *The Signature of Jesus.* Portland, OR: Multnomah, 1992.

Moore, Mark E. *The Chronological Life of Christ.* 2 Vols. Joplin, MO: College Press, 1996.

Neyrey, Jerome H. *The Social World of Luke–Acts: Models for Interpretation.* Peabody, MA: Hendrickson, 1991.

Shepard, J.W. *The Christ of the Gospels.* Grand Rapids: Eerdmans, 1939.

Strobel, Lee. *A Case for Christ.* Grand Rapids: Zondervan, 1998.

Thomas, Robert L., and Stanley N. Gundry. *The NIV Harmony of the Gospels.* San Francisco: HarperCollins, 1988.

Wenham, John. *Easter Enigma.* Exeter: Paternoster; Grand Rapids: Baker, 1984.

Wilkins, Michael J., and J.P. Moreland. *Jesus under Fire.* Grand Rapids: Zondervan, 1995.

Wright, N.T. *The Original Jesus.* Grand Rapids: Eerdmans, 1996.

Yancey, Philip. *The Jesus I Never Knew.* Grand Rapids: Zondervan, 1995.

About the Author

Mark Moore is Professor of New Testament at Ozark Christian College, teaching in the areas of Life of Christ, Acts, and Bible Interpretation. Mark did his undergraduate work at Ozark Christian College. He went on to earn a Masters in Education from Incarnate Word College in San Antonio, Texas, while pastoring a bilingual church there. Later he earned a Masters in Religious Studies from Southwest Missouri State University. He returned to Ozark to teach in the fall of 1990.

Mark is the author of a number of books, including a two-volume work on the Gospels, *The Chronological Life of Christ*; a devotional reading of Revelation, *How to Dodge a Dragon*; and a piece of historical fiction on Acts, *My Witnesses*. He is a popular speaker for both adult and youth conferences.

Mark makes his home in Joplin, Missouri, where his favorite place is with his wife, Barbara, and two teenage children, Josh and Megan, who both know and honor the Lord.